SHOULDA
COULDA
WOULDA

Resources by Dr. Les Parrott

Becoming Soul Mates
Control Freak
Getting Ready for the Wedding
Helping Your Struggling Teenager
High Maintenance Relationships
Love Is
Meditations on Proverbs for Couples
Once Upon a Family
Questions Couples Ask
Relationships
Saving Your Marriage Before It Starts
Saving Your Second Marriage Before It Starts
Seven Secrets of a Healthy Dating Relationship
The Life You Want Your Kids to Live
The Love List
The Marriage Mentor Manual
When Bad Things Happen to Good Marriages

Video Curriculum—Zondervan*Groupware*™

Relationships
Saving Your Marriage Before It Starts
Mentoring Engaged and Newlywed Couples

Audio Pages®

Relationships
Saving Your Marriage Before It Starts
Saving Your Second Marriage Before It Starts
When Bad Things Happen to Good Marriages

SHOULDA COULDA WOULDA

Live in the Present | Find Your Future

DR. LES PARROTT

GRAND RAPIDS, MICHIGAN 49530 USA

ZONDERVAN™

Shoulda, Coulda, Woulda
Copyright © 2003 by Les Parrott

Requests for information should be addressed to:
Zondervan, *Grand Rapids, Michigan 49530*

Library of Congress Cataloging-in-Publication Data

Parrott, Les.
    Shoulda, coulda, woulda : live in the present, find your future /
Les Parrott.
        p. cm.
        ISBN 0-310-22460-8
        1. Regret. I. Title.
    BF575.R33P37 2004
    152.4'4—dc22

                                                                2003017528

This edition printed on acid-free paper.

Interior design by Beth Shagene

Printed in the United States of America

---

03 04 05 06 07 08 09 /❖ DC/ 10 9 8 7 6 5 4 3 2 1

CONTENTS

To Jeff McFarlane
A man who had every right
to wallow in the past
but chose to rise triumphantly
above it

ACKNOWLEDGMENTS

I have been dealing professionally with the subject of regret, guilt, and shame for nearly two decades. And since the beginning of my studies I have wanted to produce a practical book, a kind of game plan, for anyone searching for proven ways to overcome these hurdles and live every day to the fullest. And early in my pursuit of doing just that I met Christine Anderson.

At a coffee shop in Berkley, California, we first got acquainted while she was working for a major publisher. I had dozens of questions for this new acquaintance of mine, and she patiently answered them as we talked about the world of publishing. Some years later, Christine took a job with Zondervan where I happened to be publishing my first book. What a serendipity! I was now working with the person who helped me cast a vision for what I could accomplish as a writer.

The years that followed led Christine on to graduate school and other endeavors, but it only seems fitting that she would come back into my publishing career and play a significant role in the development of this particular book, since the seeds for it were planted and nurtured by her over a cup of coffee in Berkley. Christine's comments and critique of this manuscript have improved it at every turn. She wowed me with her insightful input on each of these chapters. I could not be more grateful for my long distance friend, Christine, and the positive difference she made to this book.

Sandy Vander Zicht, my editor at Zondervan, has been incredible as always. She keeps my feet to the fire and teaches me to be a better writer with each new project we work on. Of course, the rest of my Zondervan family also deserves thanks: Bruce Ryskamp, Scott Bolinder, Stan Gundry, John Topliff, Greg Steilstra, Joyce Ondersma, Jackie Aldridge, Lyn Cryderman, Angela Scheff, and the rest of the Z team are an amazing blessing to me. I am so thankful for each one of them.

I'm also thankful to Dr. Bruce Narramore who probably has no idea how much he has influenced me and this project. Dr. Narramore has significantly shaped my thinking. Some of his writings from long ago were the catalyst for many of the ideas you'll find in these pages.

Janice Lundquist, my publicist, is such an integral part of making my life run more smoothly and making my message more widespread that I could easily take her for granted. But I never have. Janice is simply the best.

Kristin Stendera, my assistant, has been invaluable to me as I've worked on this book. Her easy spirit and competent follow-through make my life easier in numerous ways, and I can't say thanks enough.

As always, my wife, Leslie, has been the most incredible gift any writer-husband could ask for. She has endured endless discussions about this subject, listened to me talk about it in hundreds of lectures and seminars, and tirelessly read numerous revisions. I don't know how she could do anything more that would make me feel as grateful to her as I do right now while I write these words. Her unswerving dedication to me and our relationship knows no bounds. Nor does my love for her.

Les Parrott
Seattle, Washington

Part 1 | We All Have Regrets

1

YOUR FUTURE
IS BRIGHTER THAN
YOU THINK

Don't let yesterday use up too much of today.

WILL ROGERS

After years of listening to people share their own "shoul-das, couldas, and wouldas," I decided I'd regret it if I didn't write this book. Not that I didn't already harbor my own compunctions. There are plenty of conversations I'd love to do over, irreplaceable moments where I wish I could go back in time, doors of opportunities I never opened and wished I would have. If I could alter decisions I've made about finances or friendships, I certainly would. Who wouldn't?

This fact—that every honest human has regrets—is what compelled me to give this topic serious study. And also because I've seen some people poison their daily lives with regret and guilt while others have used it to propel them to a better way of living. The former spend their lives punishing themselves for something they didn't do or feel they should have done differently. "If only I'd taken my education more seriously," they say. "If only I would have talked to my dad before he died." "If only I would have taken that job in Phoenix." "If only. . ." Whether it's over the road not taken or the one taken too long, if-onlys can hound a person to death. Literally.

Which leads me to an extremely important question: At the end of your life, will you look back over time and be content with how you spent your days, or will you wrestle with regrets? Let me pose the same question this way: Will you survey your days, your months, your years, and find comfort and grace, or will you battle a nagging conscience for bemoaning what could have been?

> *Regret is an appalling waste of energy; you can't build on it. It's only good for wallowing in.*
>
> KATHERINE MANSFIELD

Confronting this crucial question can be pivotal to your life. For how you will eventually answer it is determined by whether or not you—right now—are learning from your past to free yourself for your future. Once you give this question serious consideration, the truth of its message stares you in the face: Either your past is serving as a springboard to a better tomorrow, or it is the proverbial albatross keeping you from moving forward today.

Years ago a thunderstorm came through southern Kentucky and wreaked havoc on the old Claypool farm. A pear tree, which had stood for six generations, had blown over. Mr. Claypool deeply grieved the loss of this tree where he had climbed as a boy and whose fruit he had eaten all his life.

"I'm so sorry to see your pear tree blown down," a neighbor tried to console.

"I'm sorry too," Mr. Claypool responded. "It was a real part of my past."

The neighbor asked, "What are you going to do?"

Mr. Claypool paused for a long moment before answering, "I'm going to pick the fruit and burn what's left."

His response may have been literal, but I can't help thinking the astute farmer meant it figuratively as well. We all need to pick the fruit from our past and burn what's left. We need to learn whatever lessons the past has to teach us and move forward with more wisdom under our belts and more optimism in our spirits. Otherwise, we would be like another farmer in Mr. Claypool's situation who drags the fallen tree into his barn or house, in a vain attempt to hold onto the glory years of his beloved tree. Over time, of course, the tree's fruit would spoil and turn rancid and the timber would draw insects of all kinds. It would become a terrible obstacle in his daily life on the farm. Yet the farmer would refuse to change the absurd decision because he is holding onto the "good old days" with a vise grip.

It is no accident that I begin a book about regrets with a chapter titled "Your Future Is Brighter Than You Think" because, no matter what your should-haves, what-ifs, and if-onlys are, you can make the same kind of decision Mr. Claypool made. You can glean whatever you can from your past and decide to move forward. You can take hold of tomorrow, starting today. This book will show you how.

In this chapter, we begin by taking an honest look at your regrets. I want to help you hunt them down and smoke them out. I want to help you survey your past and pinpoint every significant nag on your conscience that may be keeping you from living fully in the present. I follow this up with a few thoughts on why letting go of regret is so tough. The better we understand this "why," the more quickly we can get to the "how." I conclude the chapter with a revelation of exactly what the forward-moving process outlined in this book will do for you. And I believe it is more than you imagine. For moving beyond your past will bring you to who you were truly meant to be.

To avoid any potential confusion, allow me to clarify and define our topic of regret. *Regret is a feeling of disappointment, distress, or heartache over an unfulfilled desire or an action performed or not performed.* Regret has a broad range of applications, from a mere frustration in not being able to do something to a painful sense of loss or longing. It applies to things we have done or left undone. It applies to actions we initiate as well as to actions that happen to us. It is for this reason that all of us have regrets.

> *My one regret in life is that I am not someone else.*
> WOODY ALLEN

Assessing Your Regret Quotient

The following self-test will help you inventory every shoulda, coulda, and woulda that may be interfering with your current life. It is not meant to make you dredge up painful aspects of your past; it is only to help you articulate what might be holding you down. The better you identify the detractors from your past, the better you will be able to move beyond them in the present. So take as much time as you need to honestly answer the following questions by circling one of the numbers (0–7) under each item.

1. I recall things I ~~said~~ *Did* to my mother or father that I wish I could take back.

0   1   2   3   4   5   6   (7)

Never   Often

2. I made a mistake when I chose my career path.

0   1   2   3   4   (5)   6   7

No   Yes

3. I recall sexual activity I wish I had never done.

0   1   2   3   4   (5)   6   7

Never   Often

4. I still recall a situation where I wish I had done more to help a friend in need.

0   1   2   (3)   4   5   6   7

Never   Often

5. I have unfinished business with a loved one who has now passed away.

0   1   2   3   4   5   6   (7)

No   Yes

6. I have missed irreplaceable moments (e.g., with a child) I deeply regret.

0   1   2   3   4   5   6   (7)

No   Yes

7. I have grown too old to do some of the things I've always wanted to do.

(0)   1   2   3   4   5   6   7

No   Yes

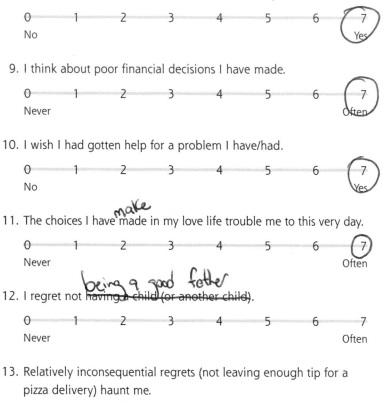

8. I should have taken my education more seriously.

0 ——— 1 ——— 2 ——— 3 ——— 4 ——— 5 ——— 6 ——— ⑦
No   Yes

9. I think about poor financial decisions I have made.

0 ——— 1 ——— 2 ——— 3 ——— 4 ——— 5 ——— 6 ——— ⑦
Never   Often

10. I wish I had gotten help for a problem I have/had.

0 ——— 1 ——— 2 ——— 3 ——— 4 ——— 5 ——— 6 ——— ⑦
No   Yes

11. The choices I have *make* made in my love life trouble me to this very day.

0 ——— 1 ——— 2 ——— 3 ——— 4 ——— 5 ——— 6 ——— ⑦
Never   Often

12. I regret not ~~having a child (or another child)~~ *being a good father*.

0 ——— 1 ——— 2 ——— 3 ——— 4 ——— 5 ——— 6 ——— 7
Never   Often

13. Relatively inconsequential regrets (not leaving enough tip for a pizza delivery) haunt me.

0 ——— 1 ——— ② ——— 3 ——— 4 ——— 5 ——— 6 ——— 7
Never   Often

14. I think about how my life would be better if I had taken an opportunity I passed up.

0 ——— 1 ——— 2 ——— 3 ——— 4 ——— ⑤ ——— 6 ——— 7
Never   Often

15. I wish I had worked at being more assertive.

0 ——— 1 ——— 2 ——— 3 ——— 4 ——— 5 ——— 6 ——— ⑦
Never   Often

16. I wasted years of my life with destructive behavior such as drugs or alcohol.

0 —— 1 —— 2 —— 3 —— 4 —— 5 —— 6 —— (7)
No   Yes

17. I have focused too much on my career and not enough on my relationships.

0 —— 1 —— 2 —— 3 —— 4 —— 5 —— 6 —— (7)
No   Yes

18. I can think of a specific opportunity I didn't take because it seemed too risky and now I wish I had taken it.

(0) —— 1 —— 2 —— 3 —— 4 —— 5 —— 6 —— 7
Never   Often

19. The hurtful words I said to someone still haunt me.

0 —— 1 —— 2 —— 3 —— 4 —— 5 —— 6 —— (7)
Never   Often

20. I never learned to do a certain activity (e.g., play the piano, swim, speak French, etc.), and I still think about it.

0 —— 1 —— 2 —— 3 —— 4 —— (5) —— 6 —— 7
Never   Often

Scoring

To find your test score, add the numbers you have circled (be sure that you have answered each item). A total score of 140 is possible, and the scale that follows will help you interpret your results.

0–35 Count your blessings. Relative to most other people, you have very few, if any regrets. On second thought, this also raises a caution flag. Perhaps you are so determined to live your life without regrets that you have ignored any potential for feeling compunction. If so, this could lead to a major regret down the line since it has required you to discount other people's feelings and perceptions. For this reason, if you are scoring especially low (in the single digits), you may want to retake the test after doing a bit more soul searching.

36–70 You know what it's like to be troubled by a few regrets, but you're certainly not in the worst of situations. You probably have a few miscellaneous areas where you wish you had done something different or you may have one area in particular that is troublesome on occasion. You can still benefit from a few pointers for getting a grip on regret.

71–105 You have your work cut out for you. You have several areas in your life that are weighing heavy with regrets. At times you even feel ashamed. Perhaps you have made poor choices that won't let you go or maybe you neglected opportunities that could have afforded a better life. Whatever the source, you have kicked yourself too often for something you did or didn't do and it is time to move on. In the chapters that follow, you will gain a new game plan for becoming released from your past and creating a better future.

106–140 Unfortunately, you are up against a full-throttle, no-holds-barred bundle of regrets that are weighing you down in countless ways. You are plagued by if-onlys. Your past is dictating your future. Your regrets have lingered far too long and have evolved into guilt over not only what you have done but who you have become. Your shroud of shame envelopes your personality, and it is time you break free from the cocoon you have made of your emotions. Consider this book your roadmap for doing just this.

Why the Rut of Regret Keeps Us Stuck So Long

Imagine a colony of grubs living on the bottom of a swamp. Every once in a while, one of these grubs is inclined to climb a leaf stem to the surface. Then he disappears above the surface and never returns. All the grubs wonder why this is so and what it must be like up there, so they counsel among themselves and agree that the next one who goes up will come back and tell the others.

Not long after that, one of the grubs feels the urge and climbs that leaf stem and goes out above the surface onto a lily pad. And there in the warmth of the sun, he falls asleep. While he sleeps, the carapace of the tiny creature breaks open, and out of the grub comes a magnificent dragonfly with beautiful, wide, rainbow-hued, iridescent wings. He spreads those wings and flies, soaring out over those waters. But then he remembers the commitment he has made to those behind, yet now he knows he cannot return. They would not recognize him if he did, and beyond that, he could not live again in the place where he started.

> *Regret for the things we did can be tempered by time; it is regret for the things we did not do that is inconsolable.*
> SIDNEY J. HARRIS

Like the lowly grub, each of us fears what is beyond our current circumstances. There is comfort in knowing what to expect, even if it is not as good as we think it could be. The power of this innate desire to hold on to what we know can compel a mistreated or abused person to put up with misery in order to have the payoff of knowing what's coming. So it stands to reason that, when we wallow in regret, we fear what would happen if we were to let it go. That's why so many of us hold on to regret for so long.

When I was in college, I had a friend who tried out for the basketball team during his freshman year. It was his dream to play ball on the very court where both his father and older brother had played. Unfortunately, all his training and disciplined practice didn't pay off. He didn't make the team and was devastated and embarrassed. His sophomore year, he tried again and made the junior varsity team where he did pretty well in nearly everyone's eyes but his own. In fact, the next season the coach gave him a space on the varsity team. But he turned it down, arguing that he would rather have more court time by staying on the junior varsity team. Truth is, he feared becoming a varsity benchwarmer, so he passed up his dream opportunity to play in the big leagues. Like the grubs still at the bottom of the swamp, my friend settled for something safer and missed out on what might have been. I can tell you that he regrets it even to this day.

> Show me a person without regret, and I'll show you a person with memory loss.
>
> GARRISON KEILLOR

Perhaps my college friend would have ended up sitting at the end of the bench if he had taken the opportunity he had. Maybe he saved himself further disappointment. But what if he didn't? What if he allowed his fear of failure to keep him from reaching something that would have changed the course of his life? Millions of sports fans are glad Michael Jordan didn't give into this temptation. After all, arguably the greatest basketball player ever, he didn't even make the varsity team in high school! Think of the treasure that would have been lost if Michael would have allowed fear to keep him from moving forward.

It doesn't matter if you are an athlete, a stay-at-home mom, a business executive, a teacher, or anything else—

staying in your comfort zone of what is will likely rob you of what could be.

While earning my doctoral degree in psychology, one of my professor's painted an image I've always remembered. She told me that we crucify ourselves between two thieves: regret for yesterday and fear of tomorrow. And through the years, I've discovered just what she meant. I have seen too many people stuck in the rut of regret because they fear what the future might bring. If they were to let go of what they already know, even if it tortures them with regret and guilt, they don't know exactly where that would take them. So they settle for something less, even the bottom of a swamp.

Again, like the grub, we can't see what life would be like if we were to let go of our should-haves, what-ifs, and if-onlys. But like the dragonfly who gains a new perspective, we can reach beyond where our past has brought us and enjoy the glory of a better day. We can move forward. In fact, we *must* move forward—our futures depend on it.

Moving Forward Matters More Than You Know

Some time ago my wife, Leslie, and I came upon a listing of the hundred greatest movies ever made. Perhaps you've seen it too. It motivated us to rent a few classics we had never considered before. And I'm glad we did. *On the Waterfront,* the 1954 film starring Marlon Brando as a former boxer named Terry Malloy, has a piercing message for anyone who has battled regret. When the movie begins, Terry's boxing days are long past, and he has been reduced to an errand boy for the mob.

As the movie progresses, we learn Terry once had the potential to be a championship prize fighter, but he squandered his opportunity by agreeing to the mob's request that he take a dive in the boxing ring when he could have easily won the fight. Sadly, the encouragement to throw the fight came from his own mobster brother, Charlie.

The consequences of Terry's choices were numerous. He squanders a promising boxing career and a shot at the title. He becomes entangled with the mob and, unwittingly, a mob hit. When Terry is subpoenaed, the mob sends his brother, Charlie, to convince him to keep his mouth shut. On a night ride in the back of a cramped taxi, Charlie begins to chide Terry for squandering his boxing career. Charlie says, "You coulda been another Billy Caan. That skunk we got you for a manager, he brought you along too fast."

Terry stares in disbelief. Looking from beneath eyelids puffy and scarred from boxing, a dumbfounded Terry says, "It wasn't the manager. It was you, Charlie. You remember that night in the Garden you came down and said, 'It's not your night, kid. It's not your night'? I coulda torn Wilson apart!"

The heartbreak of a future that has been lost creases Terry's face. Then all of Terry's regret pours out like a river. "I coulda had class! I coulda been a contender! I coulda been somebody! Instead of a bum, which is what I am."

All the rage of the boxer recedes as quickly as it had come and is replaced by the hopeless look of a man who has seen his future slip away.

Have you ever felt that way? Have your regrets ever fueled you with quick burning passion, only to die before they get you to do something about them? Deep down you know you could have been something you are not today because you chose the wrong road or maybe no road at all. Your choice may concern a relationship, finances, family, career, or even your character. It may not be worthy of a cinematic tale, but its personal consequences are just as dramatic. You wouldn't be reading this book if it were otherwise.

> *When you can think of yesterday without regret and tomorrow without fear, you are near contentment.*
> AUTHOR UNKNOWN

Terry Malloy eventually redeems himself. He gets a grip on his regrets and stops looking back over his shoulder at what could have been. He begins making difficult but good choices. Terry goes to trial and testifies against the mob and becomes the somebody he was destined to be. And that's exactly what happens when we take the fruit from our past and burn to ashes the regrets and guilt that have weighed us down—we become who we were meant to be.

Your future is brighter than you think because you, right now, are taking steps to learn from regret, move forward, and discover everything your destiny entails. God wants you to love the life you live, to achieve enduring peace, long-lasting joy, and a deep level of emotional and spiritual health.

Setting Your Own Goal

Before leaving this first chapter, I want to tell you about a concern I have for you. As a psychologist who trains other counselors, I know that sometimes people will come into counselors' offices to make progress in some areas of their lives and, after a few sessions, they decide that therapy is not working. Fair enough. However, I have enough experience to know that some people think that the good that comes through therapy is the result of just showing up for the sessions, when in fact the good comes from working hard to make positive changes outside of the counseling office.

My concern for you as you read this book is that you might treat each chapter of this book as some people treat a counseling session—thinking that just reading it is going to bring about improvement. It's not. Improvement will come after you set the book aside and work at putting the guidelines of this book into practice.

So, let me make a suggestion: Rather than mentally checking off each chapter as you complete it *(Okay, I read that one— next)*, consider how it will help you directly in reaching your personal goal for reading this book. Subsumed in this suggestion, of course, is the assumption that you have a specific goal. Have you articulated it? If not, let me help. Consider— right now—how you and your life would be different if you achieved what you hope this book will do for you. In other words, how will you know when you have reached the place you want to be with your regrets?

By sincerely answering this question in concrete terms, you will have an automatic measuring post for assessing your progress along the way. At the conclusion of each chapter, you will be able to apply it more specifically to your overarching goal.

Maybe your grand goal could be something like, "I will be able to recall the memory of my mother without cringing over the way our relationship was." Or, "I will value more deeply my imperfect self, flaws and all, by seeing me as my Creator does." Perhaps it will read, "I will be free from a secret life of sexual regrets that have haunted me for years." "I will live more fully in the present, from moment to moment." "I will feel at peace with myself as a parent, in spite of the mistakes I've made, and make amends with my children."

I don't know what your overarching goal is for reading this book, but I want you to keep it in mind as you read these pages. And I especially want you to revisit it at the conclusion of each chapter. Some chapters will have more relevance to your situation than others, but with each one, I urge you to apply its content to helping you get where you want to go. And I'll be praying for you all the way.

For Reflection

1. Complete the following sentences: I shoulda . . . I coulda . . . I woulda . . . Do you recognize a theme in your answers?

2. What "fruit" can you pick from the regrets you noted?

3. What did you learn from the results of your self-test in this chapter? What surprised you and what didn't?

4. If we are crucified between the two thieves of regret and fear, what is the thief of fear whispering in your ear as you read this chapter? Is the fear rational?

5. In what arena or in what way could you have been "a contender" like Terry Malloy in *On the Waterfront?* How will your future be brighter because you are going to learn from your past?

2

MOVING PAST
YOUR PAST

The only use of a knowledge of the past is
to equip us for the present.
The present contains all that there is.
It is holy ground; for it is the past, and it is the future.

ALFRED NORTH WHITEHEAD

An old legend portrays three men—maybe one of them is like you. Each carries two sacks, one tied in front of his neck and the other rests on his back. When the first man was asked what was in his sacks, he said, "In the sack on my back are all the good things friends and family have done. That way they're hidden from view. In the front sack are all the bad things that have happened to me and all the mistakes I've made. Every now and then I stop, open the front sack, take the things out, examine them, and think about them." Because he stopped so much to concentrate on all the bad stuff, his pace was slow and he made little progress in life.

When the second man was asked about his sacks, he replied, "In the front sack are all the good things that have happened to me. I like to see them, so quite often I take them out to show them off to people and reminisce. The sack in the back? I keep all my mistakes, all my regrets, in there and carry them all the time. Sure they're heavy. They slow me down, but you know, for some reason I can't put them down."

When the third man was asked about his sacks, he answered, "The sack in front is where I keep all the blessings I've experienced, all the great things other people have done for me. The weight isn't a problem. In fact, it keeps me moving forward. The sack on my back is empty. There's nothing in it. I cut a big hole in its bottom to put all my regrets and all my mistakes from my past. They go in one end and out the other, so I'm not carrying around any extra weight at all."

With which of these three men do you identify? I have a hunch it's not the last one. Why? Because I've surveyed enough people to know that few of us have reached a place where we are able to cut a hole in the bottom of the bag that holds our regrets. We are far more likely to collect and carry them—no matter how heavy they become. And as our burden grows, we become saddled by our past, allowing it to guide our journey.

> We can draw lessons from the past, but we cannot live in it.
> LYNDON B. JOHNSON

I dedicate this chapter to helping you move past your past. It is a prerequisite for becoming an emotionally healthy person, and this chapter will show you how to do it. We begin by underscoring the value of this life-changing step. I'll then show you the two keys to unlocking your past and redeeming it for something good in the future.

The payoff, the benefit, of this process is nearly too good to be true, and you may not come to fully appreciate it until you eventually experience it. So I'll do my best to paint a picture of exactly what redeeming your past will do for you. And I'll share with you at the end of this chapter about how to keep your past from haunting your present in the years to come.

Why Moving Past Your Past Is Crucial

Your present is inextricably linked to your past. If you are weighed down by regret, pain, and guilt over things that happened two decades ago or two hours ago, you will not be able to live fully in the present. As long as you are perpetually gazing over your shoulder, you will feel unfinished. You will feel distracted. You will feel less alive than you are. Your past will seep into your present and contaminate almost every one of your thoughts, feelings, and actions.

This isn't my opinion. It's a fact. Unfinished business takes on a life of its own because the brain remembers incomplete tasks or failures longer than any success or completed activity. It's technically referred to as the "Zeigarnik effect." When a project or a thought is completed, the brain places it in a special memory. The brain no longer gives the project priority or active working status, and bits and pieces of the achieved situation begin to decay. But regrets have no closure. The brain continues to spin the memory, trying to come up with ways to fix the mess and move it from active to inactive status. But it can't—not without our deliberate help.

If you do not take the necessary steps to bring closure to the unfinished business of your past, you will hear the ghosts of Christmas past creeping into your head and rattling their chains every day of the year. Their ghoulish voices will haunt you and taunt you until you take seriously the task of redeeming your past. You may try to avoid the painful memories of whatever is troubling your mind, but late at night as you get into bed, turn out the light, and pull your blankets around your shoulders, you will hear a whisper in your head: "I should have never let Joan borrow my car," or "Why was I so selfish with Kevin when we were married?" or "I'd never have these feelings if my parents didn't treat me so awful."

I don't know what unfinished business you carry around in your sack, but I know it's dragging you down. In fact, the more you work to avoid facing it, the more attention and energy it requires. Again, your present is inextricably linked to your past. So do yourself a favor and seriously consider these next two steps. They are your keys to moving past your past and living fully in the present. They will restore your energy, refine your concentration, and bring you peace like you haven't enjoyed in a long, long time.

Those who stare at the past have their backs turned to the future.

UNKNOWN

Before I disclose them, I must warn you that these are not "easy steps." These two conscious acts require risk, soul-searching, and a difficult decision or two. If you are anything like some of the clients who have come to my counseling office, you will be tempted to nod your head in agreement but do little or nothing about taking these steps. You may have great intentions to put these two keys into practice but may then move on to the next chapter without getting serious. Don't allow that to happen. Make a commitment right now to take action. I'm convinced that if you want to genuinely move past your past, the following two keys will insure it. What you do with this information has the potential to be life-changing. Make the experience of what you are about to read a defining moment. Your life will never be the same.

The First Key to Redeeming Your Past

Buried feelings, especially painful ones, have a high rate of resurrection. That's why the first place to begin your journey toward redeeming your past is where it hurts. Healing your hurts, particularly if they run deep, will likely bring closure to many parts of your past. Be aware, however, that healing your hurts is a process of painful self-exploration. Personal growth almost always is. But no matter how painful the process, it's worth the price.

Remember the ancient Greek myth about the nymph Pandora? Here's my take on that story: Hidden inside the box were all the painful parts of Pandora's history she was trying to avoid, the parts she had tried to bury. But those hidden and buried parts were giving her trouble. When she first opened the box, all the painful parts came storming out.

This is the part of the story that most of us remember, but there's more. As those parts were exposed to the light, as she explored the hidden pieces, she made her way to the bottom of the box, where she found that which had been missing in her life—hope. As she explored all of the hidden pieces, she found her key to gaining closure. And the same will be true for you. When you open the Pandora's box within you, you may find painful parts you would rather ignore, but as you work through them, you will find hope at the bottom of the box just like Pandora did.

Now, before you get too nervous about rummaging through painful memories, let me explain why this is necessary. By healing the pain from your past, you will be protecting yourself from repeating the pain in your present— especially in your relationships. That may sound strange, but the truth is we use new relationships as replacement parts for old hurts and old losses (a parent or an ex-spouse, for example). Every relationship, in a sense, gives you another chance to resolve issues you didn't get squared away in the previous one. But if you do not heal your hurts, you'll never get them squared away. You'll just continue to repeat relationship problems and replay your pain again and again.

Those who cannot remember the past are condemned to repeat it.

GEORGE SANTAYANA

Let me tell you how I've seen this at work in my own life on what appears to be a trivial level. If you were to review my childhood, you'd probably say that I had relatively little to complain about. And I would agree. I was blessed with two loving parents. But I recall an infuriating scenario that played itself out on several occasions when I was a child. The issue involved a sudden change in plans that meant missing out on something I was excited about. Of course, this happens to everyone. But my mom and dad seemed to have this down to an art form. It could be as simple as a trip to get ice cream or as involved as a trip to Hawaii. Many times, just as we would be closing in on whatever it was I was looking forward to, the wind would blow a different direction, an important call had to be made, a trip had to be rescheduled, and on and on. No harm, no foul, right? After all, we can get ice cream tomorrow. We can go to Hawaii next year. Fair enough. But when I got married, this history came with me and my baggage—and I can't even remember packing it.

The first time Leslie, my wife, tossed out an idea for changing plans for something I was counting on, I nearly went berserk. We were going out to eat—a big weekend splurge for grad students—when she suggested a different restaurant than the one we had previously decided upon.

"How could you even suggest going to Green Street?! We already decided we would eat at Hamburger Hamlet, and I've been looking forward to this all week. You said you wanted to go there. I can't believe this! I know exactly what I want to have, and now you want to deprive me of it?"

I can still remember Leslie's face when I said this. She was stunned, probably thinking steam would soon start shooting out of my ears like a gasket ready to blow. My new bride surely thought she had married a temperamental man that could be totally thrown by a simple suggestion.

She was on the verge of tears, and I had gone over the edge of becoming a major jerk. What was happening to me? Very simply, the seemingly trivial pain from my past was suddenly more painful than I ever wanted to admit. But during the course of our first married year, with the help of a counselor, I learned just how important it was to make a decision to heal the hurt from my past that was messing up my present.

If you were wounded by betrayal from a friend in your past and that pain has never been healed, you are likely to become highly sensitive to signs of betrayal in your present friendships. You may read into innocent behavior motives that aren't really there. Why? Because your unfinished business, your painful, buried feelings, keeps clamoring for attention. Unconsciously, you will be looking for a friend who never fails to somehow erase your pain from the past and, of course, you will be disappointed. The perfect friend doesn't exist.

By the way, when this pattern of trying to heal your past through current relationships develops, you will have created a much bigger problem. You will no longer relate to people, but only to what they represent. In other words, the new person in your life will not really be the object of your feelings. It will be what he or she symbolizes—an opportunity to work through the issues you had with someone else.

Let me suggest a few ways for healing hurts.

1. Begin by reviewing your personal history and make note of any memories you have of feeling abandoned or neglected. Give this serious consideration. Use a notepad to record your thoughts. Are there people from your past you blame for not being there for you? Who are they and what do you blame them for?

2. Next, consider ways that these painful memories may still be impacting your present. How do they determine the choices you make?

3. Finally, ask yourself what is keeping you from forgiving whoever is involved in your painful memories (a parent, a friend, etc.). In most cases, forgiveness is the only way to release any resentment you may be holding onto. And when it comes to forgiving someone who has hurt you, that's not a small order (I'll have more to say about it later in chapter 9).

If you are carrying a great deal of personal pain from your past and not finding resolution for it in the present, you could probably benefit greatly from seeking the help of a trusted friend, minister, or counselor.

The Second Key to Redeeming Your Past

Restitution. Bet you haven't heard that word in a while. It's an old-fashioned word, almost as unpopular as sin. According to the dictionary, *restitution* is "an act of restoring." And after you have done the arduous work of healing hurts from your past, the next step is to right whatever may be wrong.

Consider a straightforward example: stealing. If you have taken something that doesn't belong to you from someone, you can only make it right when you return it. Of course, restoring something, in our day, is not always that easy. When life was simple, stealing was usually related to tangibles such as hand tools, watermelons, and chickens. Most of the stealing was done by drifters or was just petty larceny among neighbors and store keepers. No one felt a need to lock their doors at night. Cattle rustlers and train robbers were members of gangs who lived in the hills or across the border. They belonged to a different category of humans. But among neighbors, restitution was a straightforward matter.

Things are different now. Life is complicated with divorce settlements, faceless corporations, legal departments, accounting procedures, white-collar crime, road rage, vandalism, war crimes, and a general breakdown in moral standards. It is not as easy now as it once

> *Shut out all of your past except that which will help you weather your tomorrows.*
> SIR WILLIAM OSLER

was to practice restitution. For instance, an effort to confess a series of lies about adultery when a divorce has already been finalized and both parties are remarried is not simple—and it might churn up more new problems than it resolves. If a person confesses his own part in a crime within the corporation, the confession is likely to reflect on other parties including both the guilty and the innocent. It is a different world from what it used to be in small town America and making things right is not always simple.

One problem with gazing too frequently into the past is that we may turn around to find the future has run out on us.

MICHAEL CIBENKO

Against the backdrop of these and many more complicating factors, some people have decided restitution is not an important concern, they leave it to the courts. And I concede to the many problems related to restitution. But I still believe restitution is an important step in redeeming your past. If you truly want to put your past behind you and keep it from interfering with your present, you need to at least consider restitution. Talk with the people who have gone through the painful process of restitution and let them tell you how it feels to get it off their backs.

I received a letter from a former student who was trying to make things right by restoring several things he regretted. He had cheated on an exam in my college classroom. He wanted to take the class again, six years later, and earn the grade he deserved. I settled for a different option and had him guest lecture on integrity in one of my courses. I guarantee he would tell you straight out the positive difference restitution has made in his life. In fact, that's exactly what he tells my students each time he does his lecture.

Then there is Peter. The day I picked up my office phone to hear him apologize for angry words he had said to me three years earlier still takes me back. It had been the last conversation we had. And after what he said, that was fine with me. I don't know that anyone had ever spoken to me so harshly. I'd never heard such vitriolic language directed at me from out of the blue. But when I heard the sorrow in his voice as he asked for forgiveness, I was truly moved. And I guarantee you Peter would testify to the positive difference restitution has made in his life.

Mary is another example. Nearly ten years into her marriage, she gave into the advances of a male coworker in the office at work. After an "innocent" dinner, she found herself in a motel room with the man and knew she was making a terrible mistake. But she didn't stop. That night turned into a series of nights with this man as she lied to her husband about having to stay late at work because of an important deadline. By the time Mary's husband found out, months later, the marriage was over. Mary wanted out and another couple became a statistic. Four years later, Mary's ex-husband was getting remarried. Mary knew she could never truly heal the pain she had caused her ex, but after some serious soul-searching she used the occasion of his remarriage to take responsibility for what she had done and wrote a heart-wrenching letter of deep apology. She couldn't restore what she had torn apart, but she did do what she could to fully own her mistake and make restitution as best she could.

Chances are you haven't stolen any hand tools, cheated on an exam, or cheated on your spouse, but the likelihood of you needing to restore a few things from your past are pretty good. Everyone who is serious about redeeming their past can benefit from the old-fashioned principle of restitution.

One of the most common but least talked about forms of restitution is found in our relationships. Think, for example, of something intangible you may have taken from someone. Perhaps it was their dignity, their reputation, their joy, their confidence, or their contentment. Each and every one of us has robbed others of experiences and satisfactions for any number of reasons. Jealousy is a common motivator. So is anger or even anxiety. For example, being especially nervous for a colleague who is on your team at work—and saying so—can steal her competence. As she is about to make an important presentation, you say, "You better be really good because we're all counting on you and if you don't do well, you're going to make us all look bad. I hope you did your homework, because this is not a dress rehearsal." Wow! You came on stronger than you intended. You're not normally like this. It just slipped out. Your own anxiety and fear only added to hers, opening the way for self-doubt—and a very nerve-wracking presentation.

She doesn't blame you, but you know the presentation may have gone differently if you hadn't given her this last minute lashing—at the very moment she needed your encouragement the most. Does it deserve relational restitution? You bet. Letting your colleague know that your own anxiety was over-amplified that day can help her gain back her self-assurance. Letting her know your words were the very opposite of what she needed at that moment can help her restore the confidence you, unfortunately, dismantled.

This simple act of rebuilding an intangible trait is what I mean by relational restitution. And nearly all of us can benefit from it—if we are willing to pay the price. Remember at the beginning of the chapter I said these two keys would demand some soul searching and difficult decisions? This is what I mean. If you really want to put this into practice, take a moment right now to make a list of people who deserve a bit of relational restitution from you. Search your soul to see what names come to mind. Then, make the courageous decision to pick up the phone, write a letter or email, or make a visit to restore whatever intangible quality you may have taken from them. Your spirit will feel lighter with each step you take in this direction.

Living Fully in the Present

Following a rags-to-riches season that led them to the Rose Bowl—their first in decades—Northwestern University's Wildcats met with coach Gary Barnett for the opening of spring training in 1996. As players found their seats, Barnett announced he was going to hand out the awards that many Wildcats had earned in 1995. Some players exchanged glances. Barnett does not normally dwell on the past. But as the coach continued to call players forward and handed them placards proclaiming their achievements, they were cheered on by their teammates.

One of the other coaches gave Barnett a placard representing his seventeen national coach-of-the-year awards. Then, as the applause subsided, Barnett walked to a trash can marked "1995." He took an admiring glance at his placard, then dumped it in the can.

In the silence that followed, one by one, the team's stars dumped their placards on top of Barnett's. Barnett had shouted a message without uttering a word: "What you did last year was terrific. But look at the calendar: It's not last year anymore" (Andrew Bagnato, *Good Guys Finish First [Sometimes]*).

It doesn't matter if your last year was a huge success or a dismal array of pain and regret—it will continue to call you and keep you from living in the present if you don't make a conscious break. But if you do make that vital decision to move forward, your past will teach you how to build on your success, rather than rest on your laurels, and—more important—it will become the springboard for bringing purpose to your pain. It will show you how to use whatever regrets and mistakes you have carried around in your sack to become a better person than you thought you could be.

> *The farther behind I leave the past, the closer I am to forging my own character.*
>
> ISABELLE EBERHARDT

Years ago, Donna Rice's name hit the tabloids in a highly publicized sexual scandal with former Colorado senator Gary Hart. In the aftermath, Hart's bid for the 1988 Democratic nomination was trashed and so was Rice's reputation. Rice disappeared from the public eye, but she came back, passionately committed to God and to "Enough is Enough," an organization fighting to keep pornography out of the hands of minors.

Thankful for the support of her family, friends, and her husband, Jack Hughes, Rice is most thankful for God's work of grace in her life: "God loves us, but he doesn't grant us immunity from the consequences of our choices," said Donna. "However, when we mess up, if we ask his forgiveness, he'll redeem those choices. God has brought purpose to my pain."

God wants to redeem your choices too. Don't settle for a sack full of mistakes and regrets. There is no need to have your mind preoccupied with memories that serve no purpose. Your memory is who you are. It is your uniqueness. Your very soul is shaped by what you choose to remember. No wonder Paul wrote to the Philippians, "Whatever is true, whatever is noble, whatever is right, whatever is pure, whatever is lovely, whatever is admirable—if anything is excellent or praiseworthy—think about such things" (Philippians 4:8). For as we fill our mind with these things, yesterday loses its grip and we begin to take hold of today.

One More Thing

Truth be told, you can make a pretty clean break with your past. If you inventory all your unfinished business to find healing for hurts, and if you make right what you've done wrong, you'll find yourself fully present today, right now. You can cut a hole in the bag of regrets you've been used to carrying around and you'll feel your burdens slip away with each stride you take forward. But I've got to tell you that your freedom from the past will be short lived if you do not have a strategy for staying current. In other words, you will need a strategy to keep you from allowing future regrets to pile up; otherwise, you'll end up right back where you started, carrying a new and improved sack of shame over your shoulder. So in the next chapter, I offer the best insurance policy I know of to keep this from happening. It all comes down to overcoming two little words that bring instant regret: *if only*.

For Reflection

1. Which of the three men in the legend do you identify with most? Why?

2. Where have you seen how guilt and regrets can keep you from being fully in the present?

3. What memories of feeling hurt or abandoned are most salient for you? How have you handled this pain from your past?

4. What specific situations or relationships can you restore?

5. How will you put into action the two keys for redeeming your past? What concrete steps are you taking right now?

3

OVERCOMING
YOUR IF-ONLYS

What a wonderful life I've had!
If only I'd realized it sooner.
COLETTE

I was on a lecture tour in Australia a few years ago and learned an important lesson from the Australian coat of arms. I was admiring this intriguing crest when I asked my host about the meaning of its depiction of the emu and the kangaroo. "Emus and kangaroos cannot walk backward," he said. He went on to tell me that it's a continual reminder to Australians that their country is not focused on the past.

Most everyone would benefit from having a similar reminder on their personal coat of arms. After all, it's so tempting for so many of us to dwell on disappointments and be filled with regrets. Even after we have done the tough work of examining how our past has been interfering with our present, even after we have redeemed our past to give our current pain purpose, there is something about our nature that wants to contrive a scenario where things might have been different. We conjure up a picture of how life could have been so much better. Our scenario of regret is typically painted with the brushstroke of two words: *if only.*

It is difficult to identify two words that have contributed to more regret in people's lives than these. Once you begin a sentence with "if only," you've sealed the deal with regret. Inevitably, those two words push the start button in your brain to have you replay your past and attribute all your current difficulties to a solitary mistake. You pretend that all of today's problems are hinged on one simple error, one erroneous decision, one single slipup. And now you are paying the price. Consider this sampling:

> If only I wouldn't have married so young . . . I wouldn't have marriage problems today.
>
> If only we hadn't moved to Kansas . . . I'd have more friends and wouldn't hate my job.
>
> If only I would have stood up to my alcoholic dad . . . I wouldn't feel so helpless in all my relationships today.
>
> If only I would have made better stock market investments . . . we could afford a better car and a vacation; life would be easier.
>
> If only I wouldn't have been so harsh on our son . . . he wouldn't have rebelled and he'd confide in me more.
>
> If only I would have had another child before it was too late . . . I wouldn't feel so incomplete and lonely today.
>
> If only I were a better son . . . my parents would still be married today.
>
> If only I'd saved more money . . . I'd have the security of a nest egg and would be able to stay at home with my kids.

If only I'd lost weight when I only had a few pounds to lose
. . . now the situation is hopeless.

Do you feel as weary as I do when you read this list? Do
you feel as hopeless as the people who uttered them? That's
the seduction of these two seemingly innocent words. They
undermine our energy and sap us of hope—as if there is nothing we can do about our lives because something back there
happened that messed up everything.
Well, I've got good news. Every if-
only is telling a lie. It is quietly making its way into your cortex and
getting you to believe something that
isn't true. In this chapter, I dispel that
lie and reveal the truth that is found
behind every if-only. I begin by show-

> If only we'd stop
> trying to be happy
> we could have
> a pretty good time.
>
> EDITH WHARTON

ing you why if-onlys keep us down, why they prevent us from
moving forward. Next I present three proven steps for getting
at the source of your personal if-onlys and show you what
they are telling you about you. Finally, I open up my trusty
tool bag for dismantling if-onlys and hand you some of the
most effective ways I know for infusing your life with more
energy by overcoming your if-onlys.

How Your If-Onlys Keep You Stuck in a Rut

Do you see how each if-only from the list above serves as a
hook to hang our current struggles on? *If it weren't for that one
thing in my past—that one thing I should have done or could
have done or didn't deserve—all of life would be better,* we say to
ourselves. Maybe so. But typically, life isn't that black and

white. Sure, your circumstances would be improved if you had saved more money or your father wasn't an alcoholic, but there are plenty of miserable people who have saved loads of money and didn't have an alcoholic parent. But that didn't prevent them from having difficulties they wish they could change. The point is that changing your if-onlys, erasing them from your past, doesn't insure that your life would be grand. That's wishful, irrational thinking. All of us, no matter how blessed we've been, have circumstances from our past we would like to change. But to think that correcting your if-onlys would make everything better is naïve and keeps you stuck in a rut.

> *If only bad habits could be broken as easily as hearts.*
> CHRISTOPHER SPRANGER

What happens is each if-only pumps a little more air into the balloon of regret, and before you know it that balloon is blocking your vision. If-onlys keep you from seeing clearly what you can do to make your current life better. They force you to dwell on the past and prevent you from finding solutions and moving forward because they erroneously convince you that there is nothing you can do. That's the lie. If-onlys make you give up. Truth be told, solutions can be found for nearly any setback, for almost every mistake. Not that you can always make things the way they were, but you can always make them better.

I know a man who had every right to hang his problems on an if-only. As he drove me to the airport one day, I asked Ron to tell me his story. I'd heard bits and pieces but I wanted to hear it from him. Ron demurred but then gave in under my prodding. After working several years as a corporate executive, he took early retirement, turning over his retirement savings and severance pay to a friend who had a deal that couldn't miss.

But it did.

He described it to me as an emotional whiplash. He told me his wife had difficulty understanding what had happened, and he felt he had never made a bigger mistake in his life. "If only, if only, if only . . . those two words kept pounding in my brain," he said. Ron was now in his mid-sixties scrambling to live on an inadequate income after his investments had drained away.

Lesser men have been known to destroy themselves in the face of problems like Ron's. He and his wife moved from a fashionable house to a small apartment. He traded in his fancy car for a small economy model. Ron had every reason to be bitter and riddled with regret. Instead, he refused to let that incident define him. He refused to let his regret blind his vision. If you were to meet Ron today, you'd never know about his suffering, you'd never hear him say "if only." What you would find is a man who loves his grandchildren, serves actively in his church, has a long list of friends, and a loving marriage. What you would find is a man who is content and happy, living each day in the present. While he winces inside on the occasions he recalls what happened, Ron rarely dwells in the past. He used the might of his mental muscle (which I'll reveal more of later) to move on.

Ron wasn't about to be defeated by his if-only. He fought it off and won. He refused to let it rule his remaining days. You can do the same thing. You don't have to allow if-onlys to keep you stuck in your past. You can conjure up your if-only scenario and look at it for a time but not allow it to linger. Don't allow it to get its hooks in you. Instead, explore what your if-onlys have to teach you. The remainder of this chapter will show you how.

What Your If-Onlys Can Teach You

When I ask people (and I've asked hundreds), "What do you regret?" I get a variety of responses: "I wish I'd saved sex for marriage." "I wish I wouldn't have agreed to help my sister move on the one day I have off." "I wish I had completed college." Or "I wish I had confronted my mother when she criticized how I disciplined my daughter." On the surface, most regrets have to do with something we did or didn't say, something we did or didn't do. But there is usually more to it than that. Think for a moment of three if-onlys that have plagued you within the past year or so. I want to help you go beneath the surface and discover something about yourself through them by following these steps.

First, identify the source of your regrets. As you think about the things you wish you could take back, redo, or pretend never even happened, ask yourself the following questions: What motivated my behavior? Why did I do what I did? What was I feeling at the time? What was I afraid of? What were my other options? What do I know now that I didn't know then?

For example, did you agree to help your sister move because you were afraid you would hurt her feelings by saying no? Maybe you were unable to stop your mother from criticizing your parenting skills because you aren't sure where her role ends and yours begins. Sometimes our if-onlys stem from simple, if poor, choices—drinking too much or yelling at a coworker. But more often than not, they are driven by some deeper fear, a lack of confidence, an undeveloped skill, or missing a piece of information.

Second, find the lesson to be learned by identifying the root of your regret. Ask yourself, What have I learned from this experience? What would I do differently in a similar circumstance? After examining some of her common if-onlys, one woman realized that many were related to putting the needs of others before her own. She had to stop saying yes to every request for her time. She also needed to learn how to say no gracefully and sit with the discomfort she felt as a result of her decision.

Another person eventually found a positive side to the regret and pain she felt over not seeing her ailing father in the weeks before he died. "I used to make myself suffer over and over by saying 'If only I'd been there,'" she said. "Now, I have determined never again to take a family member for granted or forget to express my love to them." That lesson helped her come to terms with her guilt and regret, put it behind her, and value what she has in her family relationships right now.

> *If I had known I was going to live this long, I would have taken better care of myself.*
> EUBIE BLAKE

The point of this second step is to explore how you can use your if-onlys to improve your life. Instead of beating yourself up for being afraid to accept a new position at work, you might decide to ask for help before making your next tough decision. If you bemoan not taking better care of your health, you might choose to make one health-related change every week, such as going for walks or eliminating caffeine. In other words, look for the silver lining in the dark cloud of your if-onlys.

Finally, make amends and move on. Once you have identified the source of your if-only and learned whatever lessons might be at its core, it's time for the most important step of all. If your actions or words have hurt someone, do your best to make it right. Apologize to your son for yelling at him over breakfast, then let it go. Stop berating yourself with if-onlys. No one succeeds in life without making mistakes. Ruminating over them by saying "if only," again and again, will make you fearful or unwilling to take risks. In the last chapter, I talked more in depth about relational restitution. And that's exactly what I'm talking about here as well. Make amends by restoring whatever intangibles you have taken from the person involved in your if-only.

These three steps are the best I know for getting unstuck and starting over when you feel buried by regrets. By examining what your if-onlys can teach, you will be far more likely to put them behind you. This process, however, does not insure that an if-only won't rear its head again in the future. So I conclude this chapter with a few more tools for battling your if-onlys.

Make a "Wish-I'd-Done-It" List

I have a friend whose late grandmother was well into her 90s when she talked about regretting that she had never been to New England. In all her years, she had never made that trip to Vermont to see the fall foliage. She had never stood on the rocky coast of Maine to see the waves crash. She had never walked along the sandy beaches of Cape Cod or eaten clam chowder in Boston. All her life she wanted to do these things and never did. Instead, she stayed in Pennsylvania—an easy car ride to New England—where she was born and raised.

People often regret what they didn't do more than what they did. A lack of education and not having children rank high on this list. Granted, some wish-I'd-done-its may be impossible. The forty-five-year-old woman may need to grieve that she doesn't have her own child while she learns to invest in her nieces and nephews. But many of the things you wish you had already done can still be done. Don't allow another summer to go by without riding in a hot air balloon, if that's one of your dreams. Don't put off that conversation with your father you have rehearsed in your head, if you really want to have it. Don't tell yourself it's too late to get an education or to save money or to whatever it is you keep saying "if only." Make your list of things you wish you would have done by now and discover how many of them you can still do. Starting today.

> I wish people could achieve what they think would bring them happiness in order for them to realize that that's not what happiness really is.
>
> ALANIS MORISETTE

Solve the Problem Before It Starts

On a warm autumn afternoon in October 1999, thirty-six-year-old Anna Flores was walking with her three-year-old daughter in downtown Chicago. Without warning, a window from the twenty-ninth floor of the CNA building fell toward the ground and struck Anna in the head, killing her instantly.

The tragedy was heightened a week later when CNA officials admitted having known the window had been broken since June. They said they had not replaced the broken window because other building projects were considered more of a priority.

I winced upon hearing this news report. "If only they would have done what they knew they should do," I said to myself. But it was too late. Don't allow some repair work in your own life to be put off and neglected. The eventual tragedy could very well be avoided if you do something about it today. If you know you and your husband are going to have a meltdown because you are not being honest with him about your spending habits, don't put it off. Change your behavior now. Don't wait until a crisis erupts. If you can predict how you will react when your child brings home a failing grade, make a decision now to take time to cool off before you speak. In other words, plan ahead for things you will regret and decide what you can do to avoid them. Turn your if-only into an I'm-glad. Instead of someday saying, "If only I wouldn't have yelled at my coworker," plan in advance what you will do to be able to say, "I'm so glad I kept my cool when my coworker mistreated me." Make this kind of planning a priority, and you may very well avoid a major tragedy of regret.

Develop the Mental Muscle to Move On

Pete Peterson was appointed U.S. ambassador to Vietnam in the late 1990s. Long before that, however, Peterson had served six years as a prisoner of war in the dreaded "Hanoi Hilton" prison camp. He endured unspeakable brutality, starvation, and torture at the hands of his captures. They robbed him of six years of his life he will never get back. Never. And when asked how he could return to this land as an ambassador, he replied, "I left my anger and regret at the gates of that prison when I walked out in 1972. I just left it behind me and decided to move forward with my life."

That kind of decision takes mental muscle that typically doesn't develop overnight. My hunch is that Pete Peterson had plenty of time as a prisoner of war to think about his response to his circumstances. My hunch is that he rehearsed it in his head many times. And you and I can do the same thing. We can work out our mental muscle by picturing life without dragging around our if-onlys. How would you be different—what would your life look like—if you were to leave your regrets at the gates of your self-imposed prison? The ultimate key to getting past your if-onlys is to move forward and not leave a forwarding address.

> *It is one thing to learn about the past; it is another to wallow in it.*
>
> KENNETH AUCHINCLOSS

Wake Up and Smell Your Future

Winston Churchill arranged his own funeral. There were stately hymns in St. Paul's Cathedral and an impressive liturgy. But at the end of the service, Churchill had an unusual event planned. When they said the benediction, a bugler high in the dome of St. Paul's Cathedral on one side played "Taps," the universal signal that the day is over. There was a long pause. Then a bugler on the other side played "Reveille," the military wake-up call.

I wish I could have been there. I once stood under that mighty dome in St. Paul's and imagined what that funeral must have been like. I stood there and silently hummed each of those tunes in my head. I looked across the long rows of seats in that great cathedral, which were full and overflowing on the day of Churchill's funeral, and tried to imagine what the expression on the British peoples' faces must have been when they heard those buglers. If I had been there then, I know what I would have done. I'd have smiled. I'd have looked at the people seated near me and smiled at each one. I'd have smiled because I think Churchill, in addition to signifying his waking up in heaven, was sending a wake-up call to every living soul in that church. He was saying wake up to the fact that you are alive.

One day, "Taps" will be played in the heavens for each of us as we depart this planet, but right now we need to awaken our souls to what lays before us. We need to shake off the dust of our past, live in the present, and on occasion take a glimpse into our future. As we do, we guard that final day of ours from being burdened with if-onlys.

One More Thought

You need to know one more thing about regret before I close this chapter. When our if-onlys linger too long, when they have cut a rut into our souls and we simply cannot shake them, it is a sign that they have evolved into an emotion that is a second cousin of regret. Guilt. It's that thud-in-the-gut feeling, rational or not, that we are responsible for something terrible. And in my experience of working with regret in many people's lives, this emotion deserves some serious attention. So in the next chapter, I will help you get a grip on regret that has turned into guilt. I'm going to show you how to assess your own guilt factor and, if needed, give it a swift kick in the pants.

For Reflection

1. What do you think the most common if-only is for most people? Why?

2. How do if-onlys drain you of energy and of your hope to do something positive about your present problems? Why do you think you are so prone to them?

3. How do if-onlys prevent you from seeing solutions?

4. What are your if-onlys teaching you when you go beneath the surface?

5. What is on your "wish-I'd-done-it" list? And why are these things still there? More important, which ones can you still do something about and what is your plan?

4

GIVING PERFECTIONISM
THE BOOT

Try as hard as we may for perfection,
the net result of our labors
is an amazing variety of imperfectness.

SAMUEL McCHORD CROTHERS

My first car was a Ford pickup. No air-conditioning. No stereo. No carpet. The cab of that truck was about as elementary as Henry Ford's first production. It had a small engine and plastic hubcaps. And windows that opened the old-fashioned way—with a hand crank. Nothing about this machine was fancy or custom—except the paint job. It was smooth silver with black trim highlighted with pin-striping in just the right places. It was understated, not flashy or showy, but for an eighteen-year-old, the paint job made this truck cool.

I kept that truck spotless. I knew every little contour and curve of its fenders from washing it by hand so often. And if it got nicked by loose gravel from the road or if the doors were dinged by another careless driver's car door in a parking lot (though I would often sacrifice a short walk for a more protective space), I would immediately touch it up with a little bottle of paint I kept in the glove box for just that purpose.

I took very good care of that truck, and it took pretty good care of me. I picked up Leslie, my wife, in it for our very first date when we were both teenagers and ten years later, as a married couple, we were still driving that same truck with the same paint job. Sure it lost some of its luster, but my years of washing and waxing had paid off. It didn't look half bad. In fact, to me, it was still perfect.

That's why when our friends Roger and Janet asked to borrow the truck so they could move an upright piano, I had to think twice. *Could I trust them to treat my truck with the same care I would?* I immediately had visions of scrapes and gouges along the inside of the truck bed, or worse, a dent in the truck's tailgate if the piano wasn't secured tightly. *What should I do? I deeply value my friendship with Roger and Janet, but I'd feel sick if the truck I'd worked so diligently to maintain was spoiled.*

So—and even as I write this sentence today, I cringe—I informed Roger and Janet they would have to find another way to move their piano. My truck was off limits. Can you believe it? I valued the maintenance of my "perfect" paint job over helping a couple of friends in need. I should have known better. I could have handled it differently. I wish I would have let them take the truck. And I've regretted that I didn't ever since. In the fifteen years since Roger and Janet made their innocent request, I can tell you I have certainly agonized over not letting them use the truck far more than I would have over any damage that might have been done to it. At least I hope so.

Perfectionism will do that to you, which is why it is the leading cause of regret in our lives. We want everything and everybody, including ourselves, to be perfect. Of course, nothing ever is and the more we try to make it so, the more miserable we become. That's why the impossibly high standards of perfectionism set us up for disappointment and problems at every turn.[1] And that's why I feel compelled to slip this chapter into the close of this first section of the book.

Before we turn to the most toxic form regret takes in part two, I want to dedicate this chapter to everyone who has perfectionist tendencies. Whether you have sky-high standards set for yourself or the people around you (or both), this chapter is for you. We begin by examining why this tendency creates so many opportunities for regret to take hold and then we turn to assessing your own perfectionism. The bulk of the chapter is devoted to giving perfectionism the boot. I will show you specifically how you can break free of perfectionism, whether you are expecting it from yourself or from others.

> *There is no one*
> *righteous,*
> *not even one.*
> Romans 3:10

Why Perfectionism Guarantees Regret

Perfectionism is a double-edged sword. On the one hand, it is driven by a desire to do well. What heart-surgery patient wouldn't want a perfectionist for a surgeon? What airline passenger doesn't want the pilot to be a perfectionist? Giving one's best and taking pride in one's efforts, whether it involves repairing a car or preparing a soufflé, is admirable. Going the extra mile is a good thing.

On the other hand, perfectionism is also driven by a fear of the consequences of not doing well. And it is this fear that cultivates regret. Why? Because perfectionists rarely get things exactly right. Perfectionistic beliefs set us up to be disappointed in ourselves or other people around us, given that achieving perfection consistently is impossible. In other words, the high standards of perfectionism become an obstacle instead of a means to achieving our goals.[2] Enter regret. Let me make this clear: Perfectionism keeps us from reaching our goals. And when we don't meet our goals, we're surely saddled with regret.

Perfectionism leaves no room for error. It pushes us to be number one, and if we aren't at the top, we feel like losers. No matter that you've done your best, says the perfectionist, what matters is not making mistakes. It's a good thing nobody told that to Babe Ruth. Everyone knows he long held baseball's homerun record, but few note that he also holds the record for the number of strikes. Losing, making mistakes, is a prerequisite to success. The philosopher Lord Hougton got it right when he said, "The virtue lies in the struggle, not in the prize."

Are You a Perfectionist?

A friend recently told me that every morning while shaving in front of his mirror, he consciously places his can of shaving cream, the label side forward, in the exact center of one of the square tiles on his bathroom countertop. "Do you think that makes me a perfectionist?" he asked. What would you say?

Truth is, you can't diagnose a perfectionist based on one tidbit of information. But behavior like this is quite telling. If you'd like to assess your own predisposition toward perfectionism, take a moment to answer the following true-or-false questions. Take as much time as you need and be honest.

(T) F   If I make a mistake, I feel horrible.

(T) F   My standards for most things are pretty high.

(T) F   Things should always be done the right way.

(T) F   I get embarrassed if I don't do an outstanding job.

(T) F   I am afraid of being humiliated.

(T) F   It is possible to do things perfectly.

(T) F   I sometimes feel like I'll never be good enough.

(T) F   When others approve of me, I feel better about myself.

(T) F   If I don't achieve perfection with a task, I feel like I've failed.

(T) F   I tend to feel guilty, or at lease ill at ease, for not doing a better job.

Add up the number of true answers from these ten items.

10 = IFP Score

Now answer the next set of questions. Again, take your time and answer honestly.

(T) F   I am often disappointed in other people's work.

T (F)   I am rarely impressed by another person's performance.

T (F)   If I really need something done right, I know I have to do it myself.

(T) F   I've been let down by people numerous times.

(T) F   I tend to complain a lot.

T   F   If there is something wrong, I typically find it.

T   F   I get frustrated when I delegate and often end up doing the job myself.

 T   F   People sometimes feel my expectations are too high.

T (F)   I sometimes feel I'd be better off if I expected nothing from others.

T   F   I tend to be critical about important things.

Once again, add up the number of true answers from this set of items.

_4_ = EFP Score

Interpreting your score.

If your IFP score is five or higher, this is a pretty good indication that you struggle with Internally Focused Perfectionism, the kind that places extremely high standards on yourself. If your EFP score is five or higher this is a pretty good indication that you struggle with Externally Focused Perfectionism, the kind that places extremely high standards on others. Of course, it is possible that your IFP and your EFP are both a five or higher. In any case, the remainder of this chapter is dedicated to helping you move beyond the pitfalls of perfectionism.

When You Expect Perfection from Yourself

Gwen, an administrative assistant to the president of a non-profit organization, had been working diligently to coordinate an elegant dinner party for a few of the company's top donors. It was a chance for the president of the company to say thank you for a successful year and to acknowledge their generous gifts. Everything was going smoothly as the guests were arriving and enjoying hors d'oeuvres before being seated at the dining room table. The room temperature, the lighting, and the background music were just right. The hors d'oeuvres were exquisite. Gwen was thinking it couldn't go much better until her boss asked about the Campbells: "I wonder why they haven't arrived yet."

Gwen was struck with panic. She reviewed her invitation list and didn't find them there. "How could I be so stupid?" she moaned. "I remember you questioning whether they should be on the list but—I'm an idiot!—I should have asked you again."

> *I am careful not to confuse excellence with perfection. Excellence, I can reach for; perfection is God's business.*
>
> MICHAEL J. FOX

Her boss suggested she was overreacting and quickly told her it wasn't a big deal. "I remember now that I wanted to take the Campbells out separately since their gift is really for next year," he explained. "So don't give it a second thought, Gwen, this is really for the best."

But she *did* give it a second thought. Gwen agonized over it all evening. *Why didn't I review the guest list with him one last time?* she kept muttering to herself. She was up half the night worrying about it. Gwen, you see, is an inwardly focused perfectionist. She finds errors completely unacceptable. Like many, she worries about what other people think of her and has difficulty allowing herself to be human. In her mind, it is acceptable for other people to make mistakes, but it is not acceptable for *her* to make mistakes.

Do you know this feeling? Have you set your expectations for yourself so high that there's no room for error? Do your self-imposed standards ensure disappointment with yourself? If so, you are living a lie that says "I must be perfect." And you are undoubtedly feeling inferior.[3] Of course, we all feel inadequate to one degree or another. Renowned psychologist Alfred Adler said it succinctly, "To be human is to feel inferior." Some of us cope with our feelings of inferiority by facing up to and accepting our imperfections. We do our best and try to improve. But for those of us who are inwardly focused perfectionists, we struggle with these feelings by overcorrecting and trying to be, well, perfect.

> *Aim for success, not perfection. Never give up your right to be wrong, because then you will lose the ability to learn new things and move forward with your life.*
>
> DAVID M. BURNS

So what's an inwardly focused perfectionist to do? First, you need to recognize that you are creating a no-win scenario. When you attain the high goals you set, you will tell yourself it was no big deal: "That's nothing; it's simply what I should do." If you fall short of the same goal, you say, "I can't do anything right. What's wrong with me?" Either way, you never win. You rarely give yourself a minute to feel good. So my first word of advice to you is to celebrate when something goes well. Don't take it for granted or slough it off. Pat yourself on the back the next time you succeed. Put a stake in the ground to remember your accomplishment.

You know being perfect is impossible, but you think that if you lower your standards you won't accomplish anything or you won't be good enough. It's simply not true. Trust me, I know. I have battled plenty of my own internally high standards. I'm the first to confess I can be self-critical. Two months ago while driving to the airport in Seattle to pick up friends I was eager to see, I got a speeding ticket for going ten miles over the speed limit. You would have thought I had committed the unpardonable sin. "I have a perfect driving record," I told my wife, "I can't believe I've ruined it." I pounded my fist on the steering wheel. "Do you know what this is going to do to our insurance rates?" The rest of the day I allowed a heavy cloud to hang over my head because of this ticket and wanting a perfect driving record. I knew in my mind this was unreasonable, but my emotions didn't agree.

So here's my second word of advice: face the facts. Every perfectionist needs to ground themselves in reality. In other words, don't allow your emotions to determine your destiny. Truth is, my speeding ticket didn't impact my insurance rates at all. In fact, I learned that if I go another year without a ticket, it is permanently wiped from my driving record. The insurance company calls it grace. Interesting, isn't it? That word has a peculiar ring to it if you've been around the church for very long. Grace. Even a hard-nosed insurance company makes room for mistakes. And thank God, he does too.

Which leads me to my third word of advice: Accept God's provision—his amazing grace—it's for us humans who tend to make mistakes. God has promised that each of us can "approach God's throne of grace with confidence, so that we may receive mercy and find grace to help us in our time of need" (Hebrews 4:16).

Now I can already hear some of you quoting Matthew 5:48 and saying God asks us to be perfect just like he is. "What kind of provision is that?" Well, the good news about the word *perfect* as used in the New Testament is that it does not mean to set an impossible goal. It is taken from a Greek word meaning complete. To those who originally heard it, the word would convey "mature" rather than what we mean today by perfect.[4] To be perfect, in the sense that Jesus means it, is to make room for growth, for the changes that bring us to maturity. That's the goal. To be the best we can be without being a perfectionist.

So as you learn to accept God's grace, keep in mind that you might do well to revise your own translation of the word *perfection.* Perhaps, if you are like me, what you are really wanting is excellence (a more achievable goal), not perfection. Part two of this book will have many more tips for adjusting your self-imposed standards and overcoming the pitfalls of perfectionism.

A diamond with a flaw is worth more than a pebble without imperfections.

CHINESE PROVERB

When You Expect Perfection from Others

Melissa almost always feels pretty good about herself. She doesn't struggle with meeting her own internal standards. Rather, she struggles with the disappointment and frustration of the people around her who always seem to let her down. Melissa is an outwardly focused perfectionist.

The first time I met Melissa she came into my counseling office with a list of rules her husband was to follow. He couldn't drink more than two cans of soda a day. When getting clothes out of the dryer, he was to fold his jeans in thirds but her jeans in half. He was to wipe the kitchen table with a damp (not dry) cloth while she did the dishes. The list filled up two pages.

I have to admit I had never seen such a blatant outwardly focused perfectionist. And if you fall into this camp, I doubt you have such a list for the people in your life—but you've probably considered it.

Randy had. When he drove into the garage to find a leaf blower on his workbench, he walked straight to his son's room and opened the door. His sixteen-year-old was lying on his bed, talking on the phone. One look at his dad's face and the boy told his girlfriend he'd call her back. "Son, you need to clean up the garage like I told you to do two days ago." As Randy walked back through the kitchen where his wife was standing in front of the stove, he said, "Honey, I thought I told you when you are cooking fish, you've got to put the exhaust fan on high. The whole house is going to stink."

Finding something to complain about has never been a problem for Randy. He finds ways things could be done better nearly everywhere he looks. And even when people follow his directives, they typically don't do it good enough. He has high standards and everyone knows it.

The kind of perfectionism Randy and Melissa have creates tension and frustration in their relationships. The people in their lives complain that they can never please them. And they are right. The outwardly focused perfectionist is rarely satisfied with other people's efforts. And sooner or later, they begin to see the damage they have done. Sooner or later, these kinds of perfectionists see that their relationships are in turmoil and they become riddled with regret about not being a better spouse, a better parent, a better boss or worker.

That's what brought Melissa into my counseling office. Her husband wanted out. After eight years of feeling like he was constantly nagged for not measuring up, he had decided it was enough. And that was Melissa's wake-up call. For Randy, it came when his teenage son decided to join the army instead of following in Dad's footsteps at his alma mater. His son wanted to be as far away from Dad as possible.

I hope you haven't had to experience the regret of a major relational meltdown to get you to work on your outwardly focused perfectionism, but either way, I want to give you a few pointers that may lower your regret quotient or even prevent more from occurring in the future.

First, you've got to make amends. Your high standards have hurt people. Make a list of these people and then one by one, imagine what words they are longing to hear from you. Has it been a while since your spouse has heard how much you appreciate him or her? Go down your list and set a time with each person where you can make an apology and tell them what you know they are longing to hear. Apologize for your critical commentary. Let them know you are aware how miserable it has been and how you regret being so harsh. Tell them that you are wanting to make things right. If the wound is deep, ask them for forgiveness. Do whatever it takes to make the people on your list know that you value them and that you are sorry for the way you have repeatedly imposed unrealistic expectations on them or the way you have snapped at them for not meeting the standard you had set.

Next, take some time to inventory your own imperfections. I know, I know, you don't think you have very many. Well, try this. Ask a coworker, a friend, and a family member to do the job for you. Go ahead and invite three people who know you well to make a list of areas where you don't always measure up. Ask them to list a half dozen areas where you tend to fall short. You'll be surprised how helpful these people will be! This is important because many, but not all, outwardly focused perfectionists, are so busy critiquing others that they fail to critique themselves, which depletes them of an essential ingredient for healthy relationships—empathy. Only when you humbly recognize your own shortcomings can you effectively cope with others. The French writer François Fénelon said it beautifully: "It is only imperfection that complains of what is imperfect. The more perfect we are, the more gentle and quiet we become toward the defects of others." As a person who can become as critical as the best of them out there, I must confess, I take these words to heart.

> *Have patience with all things, but chiefly have patience with yourself. Do not lose courage in considering your own imperfections but instantly set about remedying them—every day begin the task anew.*
>
> Saint Francis de Sales

Finally, you've got to make a habit of relinquishment. If you are sincere about changing the high standards you set for others, and I believe you are or you wouldn't be reading this, you've got to give up your criticisms. And the best way to make anything a habit is to build into your life daily reminders and patterns that cause you to do that behavior so often that you no longer think about it. It becomes second nature.

I have a friend, a self-confessed outwardly focused perfectionist in recovery, who starts most mornings with a quiet moment of meditation. He holds his hands in front of him, palms up, and prays for God to take away whatever he is trying to impose on others. It takes him only a brief moment, but it sets the tone for the day.

Another person makes a mental note to relinquish his high expectations before he walks into a conference room at work. He knows this is where he tends to set the highest standards, so he always pauses before entering to be sure he leaves his perfectionism at the door.

The realization that I didn't have to be perfect strengthened my faith.

JOHN OLERUD

A mom who is trying to become less perfectionistic with her kids uses the mailbox outside their house as a mental reminder to leave her perfectionism there as she pulls into the driveway.

Perfect Grace

There you have it. A little advice for curbing your perfectionism whether it is focused on you or the people around you—or both. By the way, it is not unusual to fall into both camps. So if that's you, don't be discouraged. Instead, take a double portion of God's grace. That's perfectly acceptable. There is plenty to go around. Frankly, I don't know how to overcome the "perfect" trap without a profound spiritual experience of receiving God's perfect grace. We desperately need God's grace to free us from the web perfectionism weaves. We need God's grace to sink deep down into our hearts and loosen our fearful fists from around our compulsive need to critique ourselves and others.

When we received God's grace, we received the balm that sooths the anxiety that drives our sky-high standards. We realize we are accepted with no possibility of being rejected.

Accepted once and forever. Accepted at the ultimate depth of our being by the One whose acceptance of us matters most. And that acceptance empowers us to accept others.

God's grace is truly amazing. It comes free of charge to people who do not deserve it, and I am one of those people. I am trying in my own way to sing a song of grace by asking for it, giving it as best I can, and receiving it at every turn. I do so because I know that all my regrets are refurbished squarely on the foundation of grace. I do so because I know, more surely than I know anything else, that we are all saved by grace.

For Reflection

1. How do you feel when you are around a person who is a perfectionist, and what are the lessons you can learn from that experience?

2. Identify one or two ways that your perfectionism has kept you from reaching a goal and led to regret.

3. If you are an internally focused perfectionist, what is the main message you are sending yourself? What is one specific thing you can do to move beyond this debilitating self-talk?

4. If you are an externally focused perfectionist, what is the message people around you are getting? What can you do or say to them, in specific terms, that will improve your relationships?

Part 2 | When Regrets Turns Toxic

5

GETTING A GRIP
ON THE SLIPPERY SLOPE
OF REGRET

> When there are questions to be feared
> and eyes to be avoided
> and subjects which must not be touched,
> then the bloom of life is gone.
> PHILLIPS BROOKS

My friend Allen works at home. One morning Allen discovered that his computer would not accept a disk. Tyler, his three-year-old son, watched as Allen tried repeatedly, without success, to get the computer to accept the disk.

"Maybe there's a penny in the hole," Tyler suggested.

Sure enough, Allen spied a penny in the narrow slot and eventually extracted it with tweezers. But the drive still wouldn't take the disk. Watching Allen grumble in frustration, Tyler suggested, "Maybe there's *lots* of pennies in there."

Identifying the problem is often the key to finding its solution. Time and time again, for example, counselors have to make their clients aware of their problems. Once a client sees his problem clearly, he can then take the necessary steps to solve his problem.

So in this chapter, I want to help you wash your windshield, clean your glasses, and take a good look at exactly what is going on when the shouldas, couldas, and wouldas of a regret usher in a more hazardous emotion. In other words, I am going to reveal what the seemingly insignificant experience of regret can do if it goes unchecked.

Regret Opens the Door for Guilt to Enter

A factory was having problems with employee theft. Everyday someone stole a valuable item. So the plant hired a security guard to search each employee as he left the building. Most employees carried only a lunch pail. But every day at closing time, one man took a wheelbarrow full of trash, which the exasperated security guard had to dig through to determine whether the employee was making off with anything of value.

The guard never found anything in the trash, but one day he could stand it no longer. "Look," he said, "I know you're up to something, but I can never find anything worth stealing in all that trash you carry out. It's driving me crazy. Just tell me what you're up to, and I promise not to report you."

The man shrugged and said, "Wheelbarrows. I'm taking wheelbarrows."

Regret is like the brazen camouflage of the wheelbarrows. We see it. We know it is there. And we suspect we are missing something because of it. Why? Because just under the radar of regret is a toxic emotion that secretly steals our serenity. It ushers in an emotion that robs us of peace. The emotion? It's guilt. As regrets come and go, guilt surreptitiously passes under our nose to do us harm in ways we never imagined.

Regret exists on the slippery slope of guilt. And guilt, as we will see in another chapter, will likely lead to shame—one of the most destructive of all human emotions. For this reason, it is imperative in this chapter that we get a grip on regret by uncovering just how vulnerable we are to its close cousin of guilt.

> *There is no witness so dreadful, no accuser so terrible as the conscience that dwells in the heart of every man.*
>
> POLYBIUS

Rating Your Guilt Proneness

The following questionnaire will help you measure how prone you are to feelings of guilt. There are no right or wrong answers. Take as much time as needed. Answer each item as carefully and as accurately as you can by placing a number beside each of the items as follows:

1 — Rarely or none of the time
2 — A little of the time
3 — Some of the time
4 — A good part of the time
5 — Most or all of the time

4 ___ I worry about what others think of me.

1 ___ I believe I should always be generous.

1 ___ I feel I should be punished.

2 ___ I believe I am guilty.

_1_ I believe I should not be angry.

_4_ I take a hard look at myself.

_5_ I feel ashamed.

_4_ I punish myself.

_5_ I detest myself for my failures.

_4_ A guilty conscience bothers me.

_4_ I believe I should not lose my temper.

_4_ I feel guilty.

_1_ I am fretful.

_2_ When I feel guilty, it lasts for a long time.

_2_ I feel I am unforgivable.

_3_ I feel I am a reject.

_3_ I detest myself for my thoughts.

_3_ I feel nervous about other people's opinions of me.

_4_ I believe I should not hurt another person's feelings.

_4_ I fear something bad will happen to me in the future.

_3_ I have spells of very intense guilt.

_3_ I avoid some places due to my guilty feelings.

_4_ I cannot tell the difference between feeling guilty and being guilty.

_3_ I avoid some people due to my guilty feelings.

_1_ I avoid being alone because of my guilty feelings.

Scoring

Score this self-test by totaling your points on the items and subtracting 25. This gives a potential range of scores from 0 to 100. Although this test is not a failproof diagnostic tool, it will help you examine the intensity of your guilty feelings.

$$Total = \frac{77}{-25}$$

Score = 52

80–100 You are wracked with feelings of guilt. Your guilt meter has gone way past regret and is in the red zone of real danger—meaning that you can benefit greatly from professional intervention and should not waste time in seeking it.

60–79 This score indicates definite hazards. While your guilt meter is not in the red zone, it is getting close. And while you might benefit from the personal intervention of a counselor, you will certainly gain helpful strategies from this chapter and those that follow.

40–59 You have been ensnared by the guilt trap too many times. Guilt has probably taken its toll on you and your relationships over time. However, you are in a very hopeful position for utilizing practical tools outlined in this and later chapters.

20–39 You are on your way to escaping the guilt trap. Your experiences with a nagging conscience are temporary, and you are not allowing your guilt to get the best of you. While you do not need an overhaul, you will benefit from the fine tuning tools you will find in the pages that follow.

0–19 You are certainly free from irrational guilt. You will want to be aware of how you can help others who struggle with guilt. If your score is extremely low, however, you may have an underdeveloped conscience that will lead to other difficulties.

I am not so naive as to believe guilt can be pinpointed and tagged with a number, but a self-test can help us catch a glimpse of this illusive emotion. To more accurately examine the personal intricacies of guilt requires deep, earnest soul searching. And the expedition sometimes involves excavating emotional artifacts that have long been buried.

What Makes People Feel Guilty?

Guilt is universal. It strikes people of all ages everywhere. I have listened to stories of guilt from all kinds of people: working mothers, top-notch students, homeless victims, sincere pastors, war veterans, competent counselors, engaged couples, divorced parents, and successful business executives. No one is exempt. Sooner or later, in some place, at some time, the disturbing feelings of guilt arise, disrupting relationships and leaving its victims in pain.

> *When we make ourselves keep paying and paying for some mistake, when we expect perfection, when we are unwilling to forgive our failures, we pay a higher tax for being human than anyone, even God, expects.*
>
> WOODENE KOENIG-BRICKER

"Guilt feels deep and almost physical," one of my patients said. And she's not alone. In a survey of one thousand women of varying backgrounds from across the nation, guilt was found to be their greatest emotional problem. Some experts call guilt the "number one killer," surpassing cancer, heart failure, accidents, and addictions, because guilt is a major contributor to these problems. If we could overcome guilt, they argue, we would live longer, spare ourselves a great deal of distress, and enjoy healthier relationships.

What do people feel guilty about? Anything! We feel guilty about work, family, sex, money, food . . . you name it. We feel guilty about our likes and dislikes, our assets and deficits. We feel guilty about not spending more time with our children, about eating fatty foods, about getting angry, and about not calling and visiting our parents more often.

The list could go on and on. Some people feel guilty for feeling guilty. Others don't believe they feel guilty enough. People generate guilt in themselves and stimulate it in others.

Guilt: The "Gift" That Keeps On Giving

In fourth grade, my teacher, Ms. Condon, took the class candle-pin bowling—a game played with slender bowling pins and a small ball—as a reward at the end of the school year. I stood impatiently in line with the rest of my classmates to pay a buck and a half and receive my shoes. When I reached the head of the line, however, they simply gave me my shoes and did not ask for the money. Eager to catch up with my buddies, I rushed to my assigned lane.

A few moments later, Ms. Condon's voice came over the loud speaker: "Class, someone still needs to pay for their shoes. Whoever forgot, please come see me." The announcement dropped like lead on my heart. I knew I hadn't paid, but something kept me from confessing. I had the money in my pocket. But I went right on bowling as if I hadn't heard my teacher's request.

The guilt of not paying for the rental of my shoes troubled me deeply but, for whatever reason, I did not pay. To this day I wonder if Ms. Condon knew it was I whom she paid for out of her own pocket. In my guilt-prone moments, I half expect her to tap me on the shoulder.

Guilty feelings will stalk their prey for years. Childhood misdeeds, years after others have long forgotten them, can still plague the heart and mind of the guilty party.

Balancing an Emotional Checkbook

After dating Kirk for more than a year and a half, Wendy, a senior in college, decided to leave him for another young man. She ended her relationship with Kirk abruptly and with little concern for his feelings. "I didn't think it would matter that much to him, but he fell to pieces," she told me.

She went on to tell me how he became depressed and even suicidal as a result of their break-up. The tears rolling off Wendy's cheeks were visible signs of her feelings of guilt. She felt responsible for Kirk's pain.

Wendy, like everyone else who wrestles with guilt, felt indebted to the person she offended. She felt as though her emotional checkbook was out of balance, and she was in my office to find a way to get it balanced again.

Few things in life are as inevitable as taxes. . . . But taxes aren't limited to the funds we pay the government to keep itself running. Sometimes we levy heavy taxes on ourselves.

WOODENE KOENIG-BRICKER

The notion of indebtedness is closely linked with the root meaning of the word *guilt. Guilt* and *gold* come from the same Anglo-Saxon word *gylt,* meaning "to pay." When we feel guilty, we often feel that we must "pay" for our misdeeds. However, trying to pay off our guilt is a futile endeavor. When Wendy, for example, tried to pay off her emotional debt to Kirk, she started an unconscious process in motion that caused her new boyfriend to dump her. "Having my boyfriend leave me was like getting kicked in the stomach," she told me. "Now I know how Kirk felt!"

In reality, Wendy's unconscious strategy was a roundabout way of kicking herself. Wendy tried to pay off her debt by suffering the same pain she had inflicted. And it worked—temporarily. She experienced freedom from guilt as long as she was being punished. But Wendy had never felt forgiven—by God, by Kirk, or by herself. Wendy drained her emotional account. She wrote the checks. But she continued to feel blackmailed by her feelings of guilt.

Guilt's torment is not appeased by writing checks. I often ask patients like Wendy: "How much more do you feel you will have to pay before the debt of guilt is fully paid off?" Their answer, like Wendy's, is nebulous. They don't know it is psychological blackmail. Every time they try to pay off their accuser, it calls for more.

What Is Guilt?

Guilt comes in many forms. Social scientists talk about *objective* or *legal* guilt, which occurs when society's laws have been broken. The lawbreaker is guilty whether or not there is any remorse. *Social* guilt occurs when a person breaks an unwritten law of social expectation, like not following through on a promise to support a friend in need. *Personal* guilt occurs when someone compromises one's own standards, like smoking a cigarette when trying to quit or eating candy when on a diet. And *theological* guilt involves a violation of God's law, like placing more importance on possessions (a car or house) or prestige (a job title) than on one's relationship with God.

When I was a graduate student earning two degrees, one in theology and one in clinical psychology, I noticed that the professors in the two disciplines had very different perspectives on guilt. On the one hand, my theology professors talked about guilt as a condition that results from violating God's laws. On the other hand, my psychology professors defined guilt as a feeling.

> *Guilt upon the conscience, like rust upon iron, both defiles and consumes it, gnawing and creeping into it, as that does which at last eats out the very heart and substance of the metal.*
>
> ROBERT SOUTH

Noting the difference, I decided with the help of my academic mentor, Archibald Hart, to survey pastors to find out how they understood feelings of guilt. Did they see guilt as a positive force, or a negative one? Did they think guilt feelings came from God or from the devil? In our results, we found that few of the pastors had difficulty defining guilt as a theological condition, but most of them were confused about what to do with the emotion of guilt. And if pastors are confused about what to do with guilty feelings, imagine how confused their congregations must be!

As I worked on understanding the emotion of guilt, I began to see a difference between real guilt and false guilt, or as some say, good guilt and bad guilt. Being guilty differs from feeling guilty. Guilt is the state of having done a wrong or committed an offence. This is guilt as defined by theologians. But guilt also is the painful feeling of self-reproach resulting from doing wrong—guilt as defined by psychologists. Real guilt includes feelings that are the result of having done wrong. False guilt, however, keeps the alarm ringing even after we have been notified of the problem or even when there is no danger. Compare the two alarms with the following examples.

Melody is about to purchase a mocha latte at Starbucks when the clerk at the register is distracted and confused by a phone call. When she returns to Melody, she asks: "Do I still owe you change?" Melody hasn't given her any money yet. She has a five dollar bill scrunched up in her fist and suddenly squeezes it tighter. "Yes," she tells the clerk, "I gave you a five." Melody not only steals her drink but a bit of change as well. Obviously, she has broken the law and she knows it. Her guilt alarm sounds and just before leaving the store, she slips the five dollar bill onto the counter. Notice the earmarks of the true guilt alarm:

- It is based on solid facts.
- It signals an objective condition.
- It is heard when the responsibility for wrongdoing is clear.
- It sounds as a result of a violation of a law, code, or moral value.

Linda buys the same kind of latte as Melody but pays for it as usual. She hops in her car and drives off to work. When she arrives, she pulls the receipt from Starbucks out of her pocket and realizes that she was charged for a much less expensive drink than the one she actually received. By no mistake of her own, she paid only half the price that was posted. Like Melody, her guilt alarm goes off and she feels dreadful. This alarm, however, is not true. It is false. Why? Notice the earmarks of the false guilt alarm:

- It is based on personal feelings.

- It signals a subjective experience.
- It is heard when responsibility for wrongdoing is not clear.
- It sounds in the absence of violation of a law, code, or moral value.

When considering Linda, you may say to yourself, *That's ridiculous to punish yourself for something you didn't do.* And you're right. That's the point. False guilt *is* ridiculous. It is so absurd that it can turn lethal if it is not curbed.

A false guilt alarm does not have to equal false guilt. In fact, as Linda holds her receipt, the false guilt alarm ringing in her ears, she quickly reviews the transaction and regrets not paying more attention while at the register. She recalls reading the headline of a paper while the clerk gave her the change. *Oh well,* she says to herself, *I suppose that's what that large jar of change is there for. I've tossed more than a few quarters into it myself.* The false guilt alarm turns off.

> *To sit alone with my conscience will be judgment enough for me.*
>
> CHARLES WILLIAM STUBBS

Had Linda nursed her regret, it would have kept the false guilt alarm sounding. That's why I say that regret that goes unchecked gives false guilt a foothold—especially when we indiscriminately give into every feeling of guilt, not checking to see if it's true or false. If our guilt alarm is false, we need to turn it off and go on with life. But far too many of us run into trouble when we try to dismantle our false guilt. Like a car alarm triggered when the owner is away, false alarms go on and on and on. In fact, the ringing is so persistent that it often makes people behave as though the guilt were real. And that's lethal.

Guilt's Most Lethal Form

Regret opens the door primarily to guilt's most pervasive and destructive form—irrational or false guilt. Paradoxically, false guilt hits hardest those who deserve it least. Cindy, a woman in her mid-forties, suffered from feelings of guilt every time she tried to relax. Finally, her friends convinced her to join them for an afternoon at Santa Monica Beach. They marked their spaces with beach towels and settled in for a relaxing day in the sun. However, after fifteen minutes, Cindy's guilt alarm rang. *I am wasting my time here,* she thought. *I should be doing something worthwhile.* She made an awkward excuse about forgetting an assignment at home and left her friends in disbelief.

A man in his sixties told me about a golf game he had played as a young man. At the end of the round of golf, he was handed a slip of paper that he misread. It actually said, "How was your caddy today?" But he read it as, "How was your game today?" and wrote the word "Horrible!" He fell into deep guilt when he later learned that it was used as an evaluation of the caddy. "I thought I might have caused him to lose his job," he told me more than thirty years later. He had apologized to the caddy. He was profuse and emotional in his confession of misunderstanding the request to me. He talked about feeling guilty even now, knowing full well his mistake was innocent.

A French proverb says: There is no conscience so soft as a clear conscience. Many good people live emotionally with a dysfunctional immune system that does not protect them from the condition of undeserved guilt.

False Accusations

Often we struggle with false guilt because we don't understand the difference between true and false guilt. I'll say it again: *Feeling* guilty differs from *being* guilty. For instance, if you were to steal a wristwatch from a jeweler, you would *be* guilty, whether you felt it or not. The laws of society and moral principles make this clear: Stealing is against the law and it is morally wrong. This is the state of guilt. It is the direct result of being in violation of moral and civil law.

On the other hand, *feeling* guilty doesn't mean a person *is* guilty. Feeling does not equal fact. It is not against God's moral law to enjoy a pleasant meal on vacation, even when a nagging inner voice says, "You don't deserve this." The same is true with any number of behaviors that disturb the conscience. Feeling guilty does not necessarily make you guilty.

Janet grew up in a family that demanded she be at the top of her high school class. However, when she entered college, she was competing with other students who had been at the top in their classes. For the first time, Janet was not the "best." Trying to keep her parents from being let down, she drove herself beyond her reach. Then she punished herself by getting depressed, not sleeping well, and studying all weekend without taking any time for fun.

A perceptive counselor helped Janet see that not being at the top of her college class was not a crime. Self-image was not tied to academic super-excellence. She learned there was no reasonable cause for the punishment she had been inflicting on herself. Her guilt alarm was false.

People doing battle with irrational guilt are, by default, distorting reality. The distortion probably stems from a long list of unspoken "shoulds"—indisputable, ironclad rules. Guilt-prone people feel obligated to do something that does not objectively make sense.

Here are some of the most common and unreasonable shoulds:

- I should always feel loved and accepted by everyone all the time.
- I should be the epitome of generosity, courage, and unselfishness.
- I should never feel hurt.
- I should be the perfect friend, partner, spouse, parent, and so on.
- I should be able to find a quick solution to every problem.
- I should be able to endure any hardship and difficulty with equanimity.
- I should understand and know everything.
- I should never feel certain emotions like anger or jealousy.
- I should never make mistakes.
- I should never get sick or even be tired.

The road to overwhelming guilt feelings is paved with an infinite variety of shoulds. The shear number of shoulds increases the chances of violations, which produce not only regret but guilt. By multiplying self-imposed rules, people are, in a sense, sowing the seeds of *oughts, musts,* and *shoulds.* These weeds grow out of control and destroy the good vegetation. Our minds, if filled with shoulds, can become an unkempt patch of irrational rules, obligations, and laws.

In the next chapter I will show you how to keep irrational shoulds off your back by dropping the blame game and other self-defeating sports.

For Reflection

1. How has regret led to feelings of guilt in your own life? What can you learn from it?

2. How does your guilt proneness compare to others? Are you typical or do you tend to punish yourself more than most?

3. What makes you feel guilty most often (e.g., relationships, eating, work)?

4. How have you tried to balance your emotional checkbook when you have felt guilty?

5. Complete the following sentence: I should . . . Do you see how inventing your own shoulds increases your chances for feeling guilty?

6

DROPPING THE BLAME GAME AND OTHER SELF-DEFEATING SPORTS

Rare is the person who can weigh the faults of others
without putting his thumb on the scales.

Byron J. Langenfeld

This morning we are going to learn to juggle. Each of you
should be holding three brightly colored scarves."

More than a thousand psychologists and physicians had
gathered in the ballroom of the Disneyland Hotel for a conference on laughter. This morning we were listening to Dr.
Steve Allen Jr., the son of the famous comedian.

"I'm going to lead you through a dozen steps to teach you
the fine art of juggling," he told us. "First, take one of your
scarves, hold it out at arm's length, and drop it."

We couldn't believe our ears. "Drop it?" people murmured.
You could feel the resistance. Nobody around me dropped a
scarf. And I certainly wasn't going to fall for that trick.

"C'mon now drop it!" Dr. Allen commanded. One by one, we reluctantly released our scarves, and they fluttered to the carpeted ballroom floor.

"There now, doesn't that feel better?" asked Dr. Allen. "You have gotten your mistake over with. This is the first critical step in learning to juggle. We call it the guilt-free drop."

I could feel the tension roll off my shoulders. *I'm allowed to make mistakes,* I thought. *I don't have to be a perfect juggler.*

Of course, Dr. Allen's lesson can be applied to more than just juggling. It applies to all of us who have ever wrestled with regret, guilt, or shame. It applies to all of us who have ever blamed ourselves for not being perfect. Truth be told, everyone suffers from needless self-blame. When we fall short of raising the "perfect" child, when we get a C on a test, when a colleague is promoted above us, we punish ourselves. Our internal tape recorder begins to say, "You should have known better." "You are a terrible parent." "You could have worked harder." Or "You are a loser."

What-ifs, should-haves, and if-onlys are the pathways to unproductive conclusions. I worked with a seemingly intelligent woman who was convinced she could never be the kind of wife her husband deserved. "I'm so impatient with him," she told me. "Just the other day I snapped at him for not speeding up to make it through a traffic signal." She then paused for a moment and her eyes rimmed with tears. "I am such a terrible wife," she cried.

What's going on in this woman? The same thing that happens to you and me when we compound our little regrets with self-blame. Consider her line of thinking: If only I was more patient, I would be a better spouse—and because I'm not patient, I am a terrible wife. Do you see how quickly our if-onlys bring us to unproductive conclusions? Truth is, this woman was more task-oriented than her husband and, by comparison, came across as impatient on occasion. But she was not a terrible wife. Quite the contrary. While she is pronouncing her own guilty sentence, her husband sings her praises.

Each of us has a judge and jury inside. We are in the courtroom daily, waiting to hear the verdict: "Guilty or not guilty?" Not that the decision has any bearing on the truth. It is our emotions, not reality, that will determine the verdict. So we wait in lonely silence, sitting on our regrets, hoping our bruised conscience is spared another blow.

In this chapter, we take a close look at our internal judge and jury. We examine the most common ways we deal with regret once it has turned into guilt. And it's a worthy exploration because without it we will never be free from its bondage. If we do not understand the games we play with this emotion, we will forever lose our ability to overcome it.

> *How unhappy is he who cannot forgive himself.*
> PUBLILIUS SYRUS

Here's how our self-defeating sports shape up. Typically, we will handle our feelings of guilt in one of three ways: (1) find someone to blame, (2) confess to everything, or (3) confess just to make yourself feel better. Each of these tactics will keep us stuck. Blame, as we will soon see, always backfires. And confession, if not done properly, can easily become self-blame cloaked in a different garb. So, in this chapter, I present a better way. I will show you how to drop the blame game and find the secret for overcoming any other self-defeating strategy. We begin, however, with a closer look at blame.

Who's to Blame?

When I was nine years old, I got a new pair of Hush Puppy shoes that I could not stand. I protested to my parents, but they insisted that I wear the shoes until they were worn out, or I outgrew them.

Since I didn't foresee an immediate growth spurt, I decided to make my shoes wear out—fast! I walked my bike to the top of our steep asphalt street and coasted down the hill using the tips of my shoes as brakes. After an hour, I had worn a hole into the tips of both shoes. Triumphantly, I showed the worn-out shoes to my parents.

My parents were furious! To save my own hide, I lied and blamed my older brother. "Roger made me do it!" My parents, needless to say, were not impressed with my explanation.

Even though I've grown up, I still fall into the trap of blaming others for my own mistakes. Some time ago, I missed a live radio interview with my friend, Chuck Snyder. He had scheduled me weeks before and had been publicizing the interview on his program for days. But the afternoon of the interview, Leslie invited me to run a few errands with her, and I agreed—not remembering that I was supposed to be in the studio.

At about 9:00 that evening I realized my mistake. I was mortified. And even though it was my responsibility to keep track of my own schedule, I blamed Leslie for my mistake, "I never miss appointments! Why didn't you remind me?" I asked Leslie. "I never would have missed the interview if you hadn't asked me to go on those crazy errands!"

Ever since Adam blamed Eve, and Eve blamed the serpent, we have learned the trick of finding excuses and shifting blame. Accused of wrongdoing, we respond, "Who me?" "I didn't do it." "It's only a game." "Well, she asked for it." Or, "I didn't mean to."

Often blamers are highly critical people. I knew a crotchety man named Clifford who constantly criticized others in an attempt to shift the blame away from himself. If Clifford did not meet his weekly work quotas, he blamed his boss. If he was late for a meeting across town, he would criticize the mayor for not building better roads. If he forgot to pick up the dry cleaning on his way home, his wife was to blame. If the preacher's sermon did not inspire him, the pastor was no good. Everyone was to blame except Clifford.

> *To err is human—*
> *and to blame it*
> *on a computer is*
> *even more so.*
> ROBERT ORBEN

Laying the blame on others is our attempt to take the blame off ourselves and shed our feelings of guilt. But it seldom works. Because of his inability to take responsibility for his own mistakes, Clifford rarely held a job for more than a year. His marriage teetered on the brink of divorce. And he never enjoyed the comfort of a caring community. Attempts to escape guilt by blaming others only exaggerated his own guilt.

Confession Obsession

We love to wallow in our feelings, even when the wallowing is painful. And even when the wallowing involves regret and guilt. Something about being found guilty brings relief. Admitting guilt takes the pressure off. Being found out is an escape valve for the guilty conscience.

Every time there is a highly publicized murder, innocent people "confess" to the crime. During the reign of the "Hillside Strangler," at least five people confessed to being the murderer. People under the crushing weight of emotional guilt are looking for any possible way out, even false confessions. They are willing to purge themselves by confessing to crimes they haven't done. My friend Myrle Carner, who has served as a detective in the Seattle Police Department for more than twenty years, once told me that some people are dying to be found guilty.

Paradoxically, there is something good about feeling bad. There is certainly something good about owning up to misdeeds. But sometimes a guilt-prone person will confess to things she did not do.

Confession is good for the soul, but false confession causes relational chaos. I know a woman who could win a blue ribbon for the originality and frequency of her confessions. She takes full responsibility for any and every unfortunate situation. She sees herself as responsible for bad weather ("I'm sorry about this rain; I should have known better than to schedule a picnic in late spring."), unexpected road construction ("Why didn't I call AAA before we left home?"), or anyone's disappointment about anything ("I'm so sorry; I would do anything to make you feel better."). Her guilt is boundless. Like Atlas, she carries the whole world on her shoulders. She has caused such strife in her home due to her compulsion for repeated confessions that in a counseling session her daughter said, "If Mom says 'I'm sorry' one more time, I'm going to explode!"

Some people get relief from their painful feelings of guilt by accepting unconditional guilt. Even God can't blame them since they already feel guilty for everything. They have beat God and everyone else to the punch.

Admitting guilt on every count is actually a subtle way of denying guilt for anything. The woman suffering from confession-obsession would often tell her family, "I'll try to be better, but I'm only flesh and blood." She confessed her wretchedness continually, but she never went through the hard work of changing her behavior. Being "wretched"—resigning herself to a lifetime of self-condemnation—was her convoluted way of trying to get herself off the hook. But like those who blame others for their mistakes, she never experienced freedom from guilt. And her false confessions prevented genuine, intimate relationships from developing.

The Right Thing for the Wrong Reasons

The common options for coping with regret and guilt—blaming others or compulsively confessing—don't work. Surely there is another option.

Indeed, there is. The third option is to confess your pangs of guilt and change your behavior. However, while this option seems to be better than the others, it also has its pitfalls. Some people change their behavior simply to get guilt off their back and feel better about themselves. They care more about how they feel than about what kind of person they are.

Say, for example, I forget my wife's birthday one year. I would feel terrible and do almost anything to avoid that feeling again. You can bet I wouldn't forget her birthday the following year. And when that day came, our celebration would look very similar to other years' celebrations. We would go to a nice restaurant, and I would give her a thoughtful gift. But this time I would be motivated to celebrate not by love but by guilt. I would think, *No one can say Les Parrott didn't remember his wife's birthday this year!* My guilt would cut the meaning out of the loving gestures—and they would be simply that—gestures.

When the Israelites were slaves of the Egyptians, God sent numerous plagues to convince Pharaoh of his power and to force him to let the Israelites go. Time after time, Pharaoh promised to release the people if God would stop the plague, and time after time, Pharaoh reneged on his promise. Pharaoh cared more about taking away the pain of the plagues than he cared about his relationship with the one true God. His "confessions" and "repentance" were more manipulative than genuine.

> *We confess our little faults to persuade people that we have no large ones.*
>
> FRACOIS DE LA ROCHEFOUCAULD

Some of us act like Pharaoh. We change our behavior simply to get rid of the plague of guilt and to feel better about ourselves—not to be better people. We confess our sins but never question our motives. And as T. S. Eliot said in his play *Murder in the Cathedral,* "The greatest sin is to do all the right things for all the wrong reasons."

The Right Thing for the Right Reasons

We have looked at the ineffective ways of dealing with guilt: finding someone to blame, confessing to everything, or confessing just to make yourself feel better. Each of these techniques for dealing with guilt seems to work. After all, they help you cope with the pain of guilt. They seem to make you feel better. But in reality, these techniques destroy relationships. The *only* effective way to deal with guilt is to confess and change your behavior because you are *genuinely* sorry for the pain your wrongdoing has caused. When you confess out of genuine sorrow, your focus will not be on yourself, but on the other person. Regret and guilt will dissipate. You will worry less about your own feelings and more about the pain you may have caused the other person.

Sometimes, however, the process of repentance can seem so painful that we will do almost anything to avoid it. This was Katherine's problem.

I was assigned to counsel Katherine when she was brought to the hospital after a suicide hotline counselor reported her suicidal threats. Several months before, her family discovered that she had a brief affair with her sister's husband. Since that time Katherine, a single twenty-five-year-old woman, had gone into a depression.

When I talked to Katherine, however, she seemed more defensive than depressed, and I suspected that she was faking her depression. To help with my diagnosis, I had her take the Minnesota Multiphasic Personality Inventory, or the MMPI— a widely used true-and-false questionnaire with more than 500 questions. The test not only reveals possible psychological problems, it also is able to determine whether a person is lying.

In Katherine's case, she was. For nearly two months she had convinced her family and friends that she was severely depressed. But in reality, Katherine was wrestling with guilt more than depression. Guilt often masks itself as depression to garner sympathy. Psychologists call this technique "malingering." It is a way of avoiding responsibility. In Katherine's case, she was faking depression as a way of avoiding guilt for having an affair with her sister's husband.

Malingering is always a delicate therapeutic issue. And it is best to confront it with compassion rather than condemnation. I went over some of the test results with Katherine and then set the profile aside. "I suspect you are carrying a lot of pain inside," I told her. "I know you betrayed your sister, but we haven't talked about that yet. Are you close to her?"

"Yes. Well . . ." she paused. "I used to be."

"Tell me about the two of you."

"There's nothing to tell." Katherine's eyes filled with tears. I remained quiet. "Their marriage has always been on the rocks. Besides, it was only one time, and he is the one who came on to me."

She seemed to be shifting the blame to her sister's husband. To clarify her thinking, I asked her, "You didn't want it to happen?"

"I don't know; I just know I'm sorry."

"Have you told your sister that?"

"I've done everything I know how to do, and it's just not enough." Katherine began crying, and I handed her a box of tissues. "I feel so overwhelmed, so defeated," she told me in an innocent tone. "I keep having the impulse to run away from it all."

"What kept you from doing that?" I asked.

"What do you mean? Do you think I should run away?"

"Maybe you already have."

She looked at me. "Do you think I'm . . ." Katherine stopped and took a deep breath. I could almost see the wheels of her mind turning. "I have wanted to know it's not my fault, but . . . it is." Katherine began to sob. "I have wanted my sister and everyone else to see how much this whole thing has messed me up. It has. I've been a wreck."

"But?" I said slowly. I could sense that she was coming to a pivotal point of self-awareness and didn't want her to miss it.

"But I can't pretend any longer. I've got to come to terms with what I've done. I did betray my sister. She has a right to blame me. I betrayed myself too. I have replayed that night a thousand times, and I would do anything to erase it."

The session was agonizing. Katherine's shoulders shuddered, her chin quivered, and she cried over the pain she had caused her sister.

I continued to see Katherine for a few more sessions. She eventually admitted that her suicide threats were a way of deflecting guilt, and she owned up to her part in a terrible relational tangle. Katherine achieved some sense of peace. I don't know if her sister ever forgave her, but I do know that Katherine owned up to her misdeed. She took responsibility for her actions and confessed her wrongdoing out of genuine sorrow. Her energy for living returned, and I began to see the authentic Katherine emerge.

> *Things that are done, it is needless to speak about . . . things that are past, it is needless to blame.*
> CONFUCIUS

The greater the pain of our guilt, the more we will be tempted to deal with it in unhealthy ways: blaming others, or, in this case, going even so far as to fake an illness to garner sympathy. If we have developed a healthy way of coping with guilt, however, we will recognize our faults, repent in sorrow for our behavior, and make changes that will restore our relationships with the people we have wronged. We will explore that process in more depth in chapter 8 when we talk about the alternative to feeling guilty. First, however, we must learn how to adjust and, if necessary, repair our internal thermostat, the conscience.

For Reflection

1. Ever needed a "guilt-free drop"? Consider a recent example from your own life where you punished yourself with regret or guilt for not being "perfect." Did this self-blame serve any constructive purpose?

2. If you were to describe your "inner courtroom," what would it look like and could you identify any of the faces in the jury?

3. Take a moment to inventory your blame quotient. If you are going to lay blame, is there a particular person in your life who gets the brunt of it? What does this tell you about your tendency to blame?

4. Would you consider yourself a "trigger-happy confessor"? Do you have confession obsession, or do you know someone who does? Why would someone take so much responsibility, and how do you believe it impacts their relationships?

5. Do you agree that confession can be a means to simply feel better? Have you ever seen someone confess simply to get the guilt off his back but not to change his attitude or his behavior? What were the results?

6. Consider a personal example of confession and how it improved your relationships. Or think of one that may have been reported in the local or national news. What can you learn from confession that is done for the right reasons?

7

REPAIRING YOUR
INTERNAL THERMOSTAT

A lot of people mistake a short memory
for a clear conscience.
DOUG LARSON

Children lined up in the cafeteria of a religious school for lunch. At the head of the table was a large pile of apples. The teacher made a note: "Take only one. God is watching." At the other end of the table was a large pile of chocolate chip cookies. Charlie, a young boy, looked back at the note by the apples and decided to write his own note to place by the cookies: "Take all you want. God is watching the apples."

Ever feel like Charlie—looking for an emotional loophole to avoid guilt? Truth be told, when we try to circumvent what we know is right, we end with a nagging internal voice that doesn't let us forget it. Consider an event that happened inside the Salt Lake Ice Center at the 2002 Winter Olympics where a panel of nine judges filtered into a room for a post-competition meeting. Twelve hours removed from the controversial moment when gold medals were draped over Russia's figure skaters Yelena Berezhnaya and Anton Sikharulidze instead of Canada's Jamie Salé and David Pelletier, the judges assembled for a review of the decision.

At first, it was business as usual as the judges sat around a table, poring over the marks for several skaters. Then the meeting took a bizarre turn. The head referee, known as a gentle and meticulous caretaker of skating, handed each judge a piece of paper with a passage about honesty and integrity. That's when French judge Marie-Reine Le Gougne began to sob. For several minutes, the wail from Le Gougne grew so loud, one official said, that a person in the room stripped tape over the crack in the door in an apparent soundproofing effort. Some had seen her crying in the same way while standing in the hotel lobby after the competition. They already knew why Le Gougne was distraught, they said: Her conscience had caught up to her.

Our conscience is the inner signal that lets us know what we ought to have been and what we ought to have done. A person with a "good" conscience is said to be scrupulous. However, the scrupulous person can feel the agony of real or imagined guilt. And the conscience may not know the difference between the two kinds of guilt. That's why different people feel guilty about different things. We don't all share the same conscience stamped with the same moral code. Even if we feel Scripture is our moral code, you don't have to be a theologian to recognize that different people interpret it differently. Each of us has a unique conscience and sometimes that conscience is right on target while at other times, particularly for those who are prone to guilt, it can be triggered by something that may not deserve a guilt alarm.

Almost anything can prick a tender conscience: an overdue bill, an approaching police car, a collection plate, or a cool glance from the boss. As the hapless victim of needling oughts and shoulds, one is left wondering what the conscience is good for. Did God goof? I don't think so. But I do think we sometimes err in giving too much power to our conscience.

> A good conscience is a continual feast.
>
> ROBERT BURTON

In this chapter, we dissect the human conscience to more accurately understand how it develops and how it works. Most important, I will delineate the marks of a healthy conscience to help you cultivate it within your own life.

How Does Your Conscience Develop?

Once I asked a large group, "Who said, 'Let your conscience be your guide'?"

"The Bible," one man responded. Several other people nodded.

I shook my head. "The Bible doesn't say that," I corrected him. "Jiminy Cricket did."

Contrary to popular opinion, the conscience in and of itself is not a reliable voice of God. Each person's moral fingerprints are unique. A psychopath may murder a relative and feel no guilt, whereas a shy recluse may feel overwhelmed with guilt for dialing the wrong number. However, the conscience *is* a gift from God that, properly trained, can help us make moral decisions. But because of sin, often the conscience is poorly trained. And the poorly trained conscience is faulty and can in no way be seen as the most reliable guide.

Babies, for example, are not born with the Ten Commandments, the Sermon on the Mount, and the laws passed by Congress imprinted on their minds. Nor are they born with an internal moral thermostat for automatically deciphering right from wrong. Rather, children must be taught right from wrong by their parents or other adult figures. To avoid punishment, gain rewards, or simply maintain their love, children accept their parents' standards of behavior. Each time a child hears "Stop that," "No, no," or "Naughty," her idea of what's right and what's wrong is strengthened, and her conscience begins to develop.

As the conscience develops, it slowly gains more and more power. The inner sense of "oughtness" gains strength until the mature adult no longer relies entirely on parents, friends, preachers, or police to know what is right. Finally, each of us sets our own standards, and we reward or punish ourselves by what we think we deserve.

Unfortunately, many of us are harder on ourselves than other people are. To prove our independence, we declare our own rules and invite our conscience to show no mercy. The conscience then critiques our thoughts, wishes, and actions with unforgiving judgment. Almost without knowing it, we become legalists—more concerned about keeping rules than having healthy, loving relationships. That was Ron Stevens' problem.

The Legalist

Ron Stevens, an ex-Marine-turned-busy-executive, sat in the tiny waiting room outside my office with three growing boys in tow: Paul, sixteen and stocky; Neil, fourteen and wiry; and Donny, eleven and wearing a Phillies cap. We all shook hands and exchanged awkward hellos. I led them into my office while Neil and Donny traded exaggerated panicked looks and gestures.

They sat down, and Ron said to me, "Well, Doc, these boys can't seem to follow instructions."

"And that's why you're here?" I asked.

"They know the rules in our house, but they are bent on breaking them." The two older boys sat silent while Donny idly leafed through a small stack of baseball cards. "Give me those, son," Ron said and jerked the cards out of the boy's small hands. "See what I mean, Doc?"

I winced at Ron's insensitivity and the embarrassment he caused Donny. "Not exactly," I said.

"These boys need a good dose of discipline," Ron said.

We spent the rest of the session exploring their home life. I learned that Ron's wife died of cancer many years ago and that there was another son, Ron Jr., who was eighteen and moved out on his own a few months earlier. Ron had not heard from his son since then. We wrapped up the session, and I scheduled the next appointment with the father alone.

A week had passed when Ron said, "Doc, I have lost a wife and my first son. I don't want to lose the rest of my boys."

We met for the next few weeks until Ron saw the painful truth: His emphasis on rules and discipline was driving his boys away. His legalistic insistence on their obedience was destroying their relationship.

The early church also struggled with legalism. Because Judaism emphasized keeping God's law, the first Christians had to decide what place laws and rules would play in their new lives in Christ. In the book of Galatians, Paul goes to great lengths to convince new Christians that circumcision is not necessary for their salvation. Following the rules, keeping the old Jewish laws, will not save you. Only a relationship with Christ will bring you redemption.

When the conscience is overly scrupulous, law takes precedence over love, and relationships suffer. Perhaps because he had been a Marine, Ron raised his sons like they were in boot camp. Laws and rules have their place. Keep the law and we stay out of jail. Rules, in a sense, give us our freedom. But rules turn sour when they become more important than relationships. In Ron's case, his emphasis on rules was so strong that he drove away his oldest son and risked alienating his other three sons.

> *A conscience is like a baby. It has to go to sleep before you can.*
>
> AUTHOR UNKNOWN

Relationships require more than adherence to the letter of the law. A clinical supervisor reviewing one of my early cases once told me, "Whenever you see excess scrupulosity, look out for emotional damage." After counseling numerous families burdened by an overactive conscience, I have seen her words ring true again and again. Legalism drains grace from a home. It kills joy in a church. Legalism finds rules for every situation. It breeds oppressiveness, judgment, and unforgiveness into people and institutions.

The Amoralist

Bit by bit, the word leaked out: John, a trusted lay leader in the church, was having an affair with a woman from another church who worked in his office. The congregation reacted with shock and anger. The pastor and several elders visited John to confront him with his sinful behavior. But John was unrepentant. He saw nothing wrong with what he'd been doing. After all, he said, they were both adults, and they weren't hurting anyone. In fact, he felt he was spiritually stronger because of the intimacy he and his lover had enjoyed!

John is an amoralist. He has no sense of right or wrong. Even though his affair destroyed two families, devastated a loyal wife and three children, and damaged his church, he refused to admit that he had done anything wrong.

People like John who have never developed an adequate conscience have *superego lacunae,* meaning "holes in the conscience." They perform all sorts of antisocial acts and suffer no remorse or guilt. When Charlie Starkweather went on a cross-country shooting spree in the 1950s, killing fourteen innocent victims, he told a jury, "It was just like shootin' rabbits!" And a few years ago when Eric Harris and Dylan Kleebold began planning a massacre at their high school in Littleton, Colorado, that eventually killed thirteen students, they compared their shootings to playing a video game.

However, the problem of a conscience with holes is not limited to sociopaths. Many experts believe society is breeding an unhealthy respect for "getting away with it." They point to the cheating epidemic that is sweeping America as a primary example. People are cheating because "everyone is doing it" or as a way of "getting even." We have almost grown accustomed to reading about business leaders, television evangelists, and government officials who have cheated, told bold-faced lies, and felt no pain of guilt. The unimaginable recent corporate abuse that began with the corporation Enron in

2002 set off a series of corporate scandals that revealed leaders who thought they could get away with it.

The Healthy Conscience

People with a healthy conscience seldom show up in my office, but I can remember a college student who came to me to clear her conscience—and changed her life as a result.

The first time Trudy showed up in my office, she refused to look at me. Her hair was shaggy and unkempt, and she wore a t-shirt and faded jeans that were far too tight for her large figure. Her supervisor from nursing school had recommended that Trudy see me, for she was failing every course and did not get along with the other nurses. But Trudy refused to open up to me.

> *A good conscience is to the soul what health is to the body; it preserves constant ease and serenity within us.*
> Joseph Addison

After talking in circles for a while, I stopped the conversation. "I can understand why you don't feel like talking to me," I said, "but I doubt if things are going to improve if you refuse to talk about your problems." She looked startled, but I continued, "Feel free to leave, but if there comes a time when you are willing to level with me, call for an appointment, and I'll be glad to see you."

She left, but a few days later she came back. And this time her attitude was different. She had come of her own volition. And she was ready to talk. This time she told me a long, sad story about an unsavory relationship with an older man who had taken advantage of her. As a result, she was dying inside from the pain of guilt.

I listened carefully as she told her story. Then I told her she could be forgiven—that if she repented of her behavior, she could go on with her life and make changes for the better. Six weeks later, Trudy's supervisor called me to report that the young woman had done a complete turnaround. "She is happy with school," the supervisor said. "Her class work has improved considerably, and so have her relationships with the other students. She will be staying in school, and I believe she will graduate and make a fine nurse."

Trudy suffered from the pain of guilt, a pain no less severe than actual physical pain. But physical pain is necessary to our survival, as Dr. Paul Brand demonstrates in his book *Pain: The Gift Nobody Wants*. In his work with lepers, Dr. Brand discovered that lepers were not able to feel pain in their extremities. Without the danger signal of pain, lepers repeatedly injured themselves. As a result, they lost their most vulnerable parts—their fingers and their toes.

Without the pain of guilty feelings, everyone would become moral lepers. But the pain of guilt in a healthy conscience keeps us from self-destructive acts. A healthy conscience tenses up whenever a wrong has been done, but it also eases and comes back to a relaxed state when a wrong has been corrected.

How does a healthy conscience function? A healthy conscience is not bound by rigid rules. It bends without breaking. Like the gyroscope on a ship, it adjusts to new situations. The person with a strong conscience lives by principles, is guided by an enlightened intellect, and is inspired to follow ideals. In addition, the person with a healthy conscience is discerning. He or she carefully thinks through moral problems and, in reaching a moral decision, balances a concern for rules with a deeper concern for relationships.

Here are other qualities that make up the healthy conscience.

1. A healthy conscience does not look for an easy way out.

During an exam, a proctor saw one student obviously cheating. When the exam was over and the students handed in their blue books, the proctor pulled the cheater aside. "I'll take that book, please," he said. "I saw you cheating."

> *Conscience is the mirror of our souls, which represents the errors of our lives in their full shape.*
>
> GEORGE BANCROFT

The student stared the proctor in the eye. "Cheating? Me? Have you any idea who I am?"

"No," said the proctor.

"Good!" said the student, who grabbed a stack of blue books, threw them into the air with his own, and ran from the room.

Unlike this crafty student, people with a healthy conscience face up to their wrongdoing. They know when they have stepped out of line. They do not try to deny or excuse it, because the healthy conscience is not afraid of responsibility.

2. A healthy conscience accepts human weakness.

One of the most celebrated of all "I Love Lucy" episodes featured Lucy wrapping candy as it passed on a conveyor belt. In the mistaken belief that Lucy was handling the candy with competence, her supervisor doubled the conveyor belt's speed. An occasional piece of candy got wrapped, but most of them ended up in her mouth or hidden in her blouse.

The unhealthy conscience is like Lucy's supervisor, who ignored her limits and relentlessly increased her demands. An unhealthy conscience pushes the limits of our humanness and eventually breaks our spirits.

The healthy conscience, on the other hand, accepts human limits and adjusts its expectations to fit them. For example, a woman who locks her keys in the car may feel stupid, but she will not grovel in her mistake. Instead, her healthy conscience will help her to analyze the offending act or word, control the damage, and then move on with life.

3. A healthy conscience is concerned with "morality" and not with "moralism."

People with unhealthy consciences are more concerned with looking good than being good. They are moralists who always tell everyone else what is right and what is wrong. Because they are so preoccupied with the rules of the road, they don't pay attention to the ideals and reasons behind the rules, nor do they have time to extend love and understanding to others.

People with healthy consciences, in contrast, know why something is right or wrong. Their actions are not based on rules, but on what is right and virtuous. They are easy to live with, affirming in their relationships, and always ready to show loving kindness.

4. A healthy conscience knows how to receive forgiveness.

The British poet William Cowper, well known as one of the principal writers of gospel hymns during the eighteenth century, penned the often sung words of God's mercy and forgiveness:

> There is a fountain filled with blood,
> Drawn from Emmanuel's veins,
> And sinners plunged beneath that flood
> Lose all their guilty stains
> E'er since, by faith, I saw the stream,
> Thy flowing wounds supply,
> Redeeming love has been my theme,
> And shall be till I die.

Ironically, after a life riddled with loss, bouts of depression, and a suicide attempt, Cowper became convinced he was beyond forgiveness and even came to consider himself, "Damned below Judas." Not even his close friend the Reverend John Newton, author of "Amazing Grace," could convince Cowper of his redemption. Cowper died believing he was beyond forgiveness, though his hymns were used, among other things, in an influential campaign against slavery.

A tyrannical conscience has great difficulty accepting forgiveness. It demands additional punishment and tries to earn God's love. But God doesn't require us to pay our own way. He sent Jesus to cover for us, as the apostle Paul reminded the Galatians when he wrote: "Are you now trying to finish by human effort? Have you experienced so much in vain?" (Galatians 3:3–4). A healthy conscience knows how to receive forgiveness.

> *There is one thing alone that stands the brunt of life throughout its course:*
> *a quiet conscience.*
> EURIPIDES

Let me remind you once more to pause for a moment at the end of this chapter, review the overarching goal you set for yourself in the first chapter and explore exactly how this chapter relates to it. What have you learned about your personal conscience as it relates to your goal? To help you clarify this a bit more, here is a simple and quick assessment of where you stand on the qualities that make up a healthy conscience.

Rating Your Conscience

With the information you gained from this chapter, circle the number that accurately describes you and your conscience.

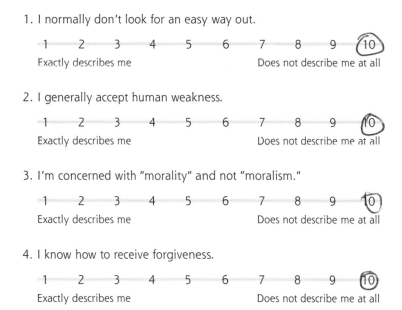

1. I normally don't look for an easy way out.

1   2   3   4   5   6   7   8   9   ⑩

Exactly describes me   Does not describe me at all

2. I generally accept human weakness.

1   2   3   4   5   6   7   8   9   ⑩

Exactly describes me   Does not describe me at all

3. I'm concerned with "morality" and not "moralism."

1   2   3   4   5   6   7   8   9   ⑩

Exactly describes me   Does not describe me at all

4. I know how to receive forgiveness.

1   2   3   4   5   6   7   8   9   ⑩

Exactly describes me   Does not describe me at all

There are forty points possible on this assessment and the lower your score, the healthier your conscience is. For example, a score of ten is better than a score of twenty. You can use these items to reassess your conscience whenever you like. For now, the point is to see what areas within your conscience, if any, need some deliberate work.

Now, before we take a closer look at guilt and how to control its influence on our lives, we need to answer one more question: What's shame got to do with regret and guilt?

For Reflection

1. How did you change your opinion, if at all, on where the human conscience comes from after reading this?

2. Is "Let your conscience be your guide" always a good principle to follow? Why or why not?

3. Do you have personal leanings toward either the legalist or the amoralist? What have been the top three most significant influences on your conscience?

4. How well do you accept human weakness in yourself and others, and how could you do this better?

5. Which marks of a healthy conscience do you need to work on? What advice would you give to someone in your shoes?

8

GIVING SHAME
A RUN FOR ITS MONEY

> What other dungeon is so dark as one's own heart!
> What jailer so inexorable as one's self!
> NATHANIEL HAWTHORNE

Shortly after midnight on Saturday, April 26, 1986, a power surge raced through reactor number four of the Chernobyl nuclear power plant. The reactor exploded, and for ten days a toxic nuclear cloud hovered over vast areas of the Soviet Union and Europe.

This nuclear disaster was the worst in history, producing ninety times the radioactive fallout of the atomic bomb dropped on Hiroshima and one million times the emission level at Three Mile Island. On a humanitarian assignment with World Vision International, I witnessed firsthand the devastation of this explosion. I saw ghost villages, gardens of weeds, and people physically mutilated by radiation. But the landscape and faces I witnessed, horrible as they were, were not as scarred as the human hearts I encountered.

Shortly after being picked up at the airport, my driver brought me to a building where nine feeble men awaited my arrival. They were the "liquidators," the brave Russian firefighters who had fought the initial reactor blaze and survived. While their bodies were filled with disease, it was their spirits that cried out for healing, and I was there to lead them in group therapy.

Each of these men told their story of combating the disaster and how they have tried to live with the consequences ever since. Breathing through artificial inhalers, their raspy voices let me in on what scorching heat and toxic fumes can do to the spirit as well as the body. But they also confessed a surprising burden. "We could not save our country from the pain," one of the men groaned.

"He is right," another said. "If we could have done more, perhaps others would have been spared."

Shocked, I said, "But you are heroes!" I tried unsuccessfully to make eye contact. None of them looked at me. They stared blankly into nowhere or watched the floor. "How has your country honored you for your heroism?" I asked.

One man spoke up. "With sickness. They honored us with sickness."

This lack of appreciation, coupled with their own self-imposed guilt over the fire that roared out of control, led these men to carry the dead weight of shame. If they had done a better job, they reasoned, their efforts would have been recognized and rewarded. But since they received inhalers instead of medals, they felt their shame deeply.

There smites nothing so sharp, nor smelleth so sour as shame.

WILLIAM LANGLAND

We have already seen that there comes a point when regret often merges with guilt. But there also comes a time when the emotional pain of guilt turns as toxic as any fumes in Chernobyl. When guilt moves from a thud-in-the-gut feeling to a feeling of failure, the seeds of shame are sown. When guilt seeps into the emotional bloodstream, permeating a person's sense of self-worth, guilt becomes shame. We may feel *guilty* for what we *did*, but we feel *ashamed* of who we *are*.

To keep the big picture in mind, let me say it again: Regret gives guilt a foothold. And guilt opens the double doors to shame. The sole focus of this chapter is on shame, not on regret. Why? Because shame has left regret in the dust and morphed into the ugliest emotional experience of all. If, on the one hand, shame is not a part of your personality, if it has only sideswiped your emotions, please feel free to move on to the next chapter. And don't feel an ounce of guilt about doing this!

If, on the other hand, your regret has moved into guilt, you're just a few paces from shame. And if you are in the unfortunate situation of suffering from a full blown case of shame, this chapter is especially for you. I want to help you escape the toxic emotion of shame and I dedicate this chapter to doing just that. I begin by underscoring how shame sinks its roots deep down into our identity to dismantle our dignity and self-respect. From there I make a clarifying comment about shame's relationship to guilt and then provide you with a quick self-test for assessing your own tendency toward shame. We'll then take a quick psychological tour of your own identity when it becomes entangled with shame. Next, I expose some common and dangerous side effects of shame that lead to believing its costly lie. This understanding will set you up for internalizing the amazing alternative to the toxins of regret, guilt, and shame.

The Chernobyl of the Spirit

Shame is the Chernobyl of the spirit, and its fallout contaminates the soul. Not satisfied to tinker with how we feel about ourselves, it changes who we are. Shame is not a gap between how we act and how we think we ought to act. It is the gulf between who we are and who we think we ought to be. It is not the feeling that we have done wrong. It is the feeling that we, our very *selves*, are wrong.

Each year I take my psychology students to a prison to talk with men who have been diagnosed as sociopaths. When we arrive there, we pass through several iron doors and then through highly sensitive metal detectors. Eventually, we arrive in a holding area where a metal gate closes electronically with a loud clang behind us. For the next three hours, the students experience life as a condemned person.

At the end of their visit, students understand that people who are condemned do not simply believe they have *done* something bad; they believe they *are* bad.

People don't have to be in prison to feel shame. All of us have difficulty separating who we are from what we do. An act of incompetence or poor form can trigger a shame reaction akin to the feeling of being caught outside with only underwear on. But people who are especially prone to shame live with a deep sense of unworthiness and a constant fear of rejection. Their fear about their worth is as frightening as any death sentence.

In theory, guilt and shame are distinct. According to Freud, we feel *shame* when we fall short of our "ego ideal"—when we compromise our personal standards of who we ought to be. However, we feel *guilt* when we do something we know is wrong. While guilt is the fear of *punishment,* shame is the fear of *abandonment.* In other words, guilt results from crossing a boundary and being on the wrong side, while shame is the feeling of having been born there.

Freud may have been able to make theoretical distinctions between shame and guilt, but in reality, the two feelings often overlap. Guilt is mostly about things we have *done.* We feel guilty when we lie about our pasts, when we cheat on our diets, or when we commit adultery. And when we experience guilt for too long—when we begin to define who we are by what we have done—our guilt turns into shame.

> *If you haven't forgiven yourself something, how can you forgive others?*
> Dolores Huerta

And shame strikes at our very identity, causing us to hate ourselves and believe we are worthless.

Recently, I counseled a middle manager who had lost his job. Already suffering from guilt because he had neglected his family during his busy years at work, he now felt a deep sense of shame because he was unable to find a new job. He told me, "If I can't find a job with all of my education and experience, there must be something dreadfully wrong with me." His long-standing guilt had turned into a crippling sense of shame.

Testing Your Level of Shame

"Shame on you; you know better than that."

"You ought to be ashamed of yourself for letting us down."

"After all we've done for you, how could you hurt us this way?"

Statements like these are all it takes to increase poor self-esteem and generate shame. If you grew up in an environment peppered by statements like these, you are probably troubled with feelings of shame as an adult.

The following test can help you assess whether your feelings of guilt have turned to shame. There are no right or wrong answers. Take as much time as needed. Answer each item carefully and accurately by placing a number beside each of the items as follows:

1 — Rarely or none of the time.
2 — A little of the time.
3 — Some of the time.
4 — A good part of the time.
5 — Most or all of the time.

_5_ I feel I am not what I ought to be.

_4_ I feel as if God must be disgusted with me.

_3_ I feel as if I will never be acceptable.

_4_ I feel flawed or blemished inside.

_4_ I feel inferior to most people I know.

_3_ I feel not only that I have made mistakes but that I am a mistake.

_2_ I feel as if I just cannot measure up to the person I was created to be.

_3_ I feel I can be a better person than I am but fear I'll never measure up.

_2_ I feel I let people in my life down.

4 __ I feel like a raunchy person.

3 __ I feel rotten inside.

4 __ I feel worthless.

4 __ I feel nobody could really love me if they really know me.

3 __ I feel like a phony.

3 __ I feel humiliated.

3 __ I feel that if people really know me they would never befriend me.

2 __ My life will forever be dishonored by things in my past.

2 __ I know others think poorly of me.

2 __ If a person looks down on me, I think they are right.

3 __ My value is diminished because of my past.

4 __ I feel hopeless.

3 __ I make the same mistakes over and over.

4 __ I feel that I'd like to change but can't.

3 __ I feel inferior.

4 __ I give up easily.

4 __ I am disgusted with myself.

4 __ I feel some things have basically ruined my life.

4 __ I feel I am an immoral person.

3 __ I feel I will never have a wonderful life.

4 __ I feel lonely.

4 __ I feel inadequate.

Scoring

This test is scored by totaling the numbers on the items and subtracting 25. This gives a potential range of scores from 0 to 100.

Although this test is not a fail-proof diagnostic tool, it will help you measure the intensity of your shame feelings.

$$\text{Total} = \underline{102}$$
$$-25$$
$$\text{Score} = \underline{77}$$

80–100   You are in an extremely dangerous and toxic shame-zone. You will benefit greatly from professional help and should take the appropriate steps to locate a competent counselor who can help you with this struggle.

60–79   You may not be in immediate need of professional help, but you are not out of the danger zone. You might benefit from the assistance of a counselor who can help you process your struggle with shame at a personal level, and you will certainly benefit from this chapter and those that follow.

40–59   You are suffering from shame, which has probably taken its toll on you and the people around you. However, you are in a good position to learn how to escape shame's scourge and the remainder of this book will show you how.

20–39   You are on your way to escaping shame's clutches. Your episodes of self-loathing shame are temporary, and you are not allowing your shame to get the best of you. However, you can benefit from some fine tuning.

0–19   You are free from shame's damage and have what it takes to cultivate a healthy sense of dignity and to build a solid foundation of healthy relationships. At the same time, you will want to be aware of how you can help others who are suffering from shame.

There are always dangers in pinpointing an emotion and measuring its intensity. Use this self-test as a mirror to view your shame proneness, but remember that it only reflects a single dimension. To more accurately understand the impact of shame on relationships, we must explore the roots of shame.

The Deep Roots of Shame

For most of us, the roots of shame lie buried deep in our childhood. As Dr. Missildine, a psychiatrist and researcher, found, we derive our self-worth as a child from only four or five people: our mother, father, brother, sister, close relative, neighbor, or teacher.[5] The way these people listen to us, treat us, and talk to us all affect how we see ourselves. By the time we have reached our early teens, we have learned very well that we are beautiful or ugly, smart or dumb, fast or slow, can spell or cannot, hate arithmetic or love it. Sometime between the years of thirteen and fifteen, this mental picture of ourselves becomes complete.

What happens to this inner picture of ourselves as we grow older? Does our picture of ourselves as children fade away? No. In fact, we will keep this picture in our minds for the rest of our lives. To be sure, as we mature into adulthood, we will begin

> *When you make a world tolerable for yourself, you make a world tolerable for others.*
>
> ANAIS NIN

to wrap that inner child with the trappings of adulthood: education, families of our own, careers. But underneath all the adult sophistication lies our self-concept. We may be six feet tall, sitting behind an important desk, or have the figure of a fashion model, but deep in our psyches we are dominated by the attitudes we acquired as children.

Our original mental picture of ourselves, as Dr. Missildine suggests, is the work of all the people whose opinions influenced how we saw ourselves. But these people may have been wrong. They may have labeled us as slow or stupid. They may have disciplined us too harshly, or they may have not disciplined us enough. They may have even abused us verbally, emotionally, physically, or sexually. And their mistreatment damaged us to the point where we began to feel a deep sense of shame for being who we are.

> *Self-esteem*
> *is the reputation*
> *we acquire*
> *with ourselves.*
>
> NATHANIEL BRANDEN

None of us can emerge from childhood without feeling defective somehow. But if you are relentlessly hounded by shame, the roots of your struggles can invariably be traced to the inner child of your past, who did not receive the proper love and care needed to form a strong self-image.

Obviously, you cannot change what happened to you as a child. But the next two chapters will show you how to deal with guilt before it turns into crippling shame. Before moving ahead, however, let's look at the side effects of shame and expose shame's most debilitating lie.

The Side Effects of Shame

Shame can destroy us emotionally. Not only does it eat away at the very core of our identity, it is accompanied by some terrible side effects. Here's a quick look at some of the most common problems associated with shame.

Feelings of Inadequacy

A friend showed me a cartoon of two cows in a pasture watching as a milk truck passes by. On the side of the truck are the words, "Pasteurized, homogenized, standardized, Vitamin A added." One cow sighs and says to the other, "Kinda makes you feel inadequate, doesn't it?"

Like the cows, people prone to shame feel a deep sense of inadequacy that eats away at their self-worth. Their feelings of inadequacy expand into feelings of inferiority and worthlessness. Shame-prone people begin to discount their own value.

Feelings of Rejection

The film *The Joy Luck Club,* based on Amy Tan's novel, is about the strained relationships between four Chinese-born mothers and their adult American-born daughters. As the daughters mature, the mothers' expectations of how a woman should live conflict with the values and goals of their American daughters.

In one scene, June and her mother are cleaning up after a dinner party. The mother notices that June is upset. During the party, June felt slighted by her mother. Her mother asks, "So it's me you're mad at?"

Defensive, June responds, "No, I'm just sorry that you got stuck with such a loser, that I've always been so disappointing."

"What do you mean 'disappoint'?"

June shakes her head and lists her failures: "Everything. My grades. My job. Not getting married. Everything you expected of me."

Her mother answers defensively, "Not expect anything. Never expect. Only hope. Only hope the best for you. It's not wrong to hope."

June blurts out, "No, well, it hurts. Because every time you hoped for something I couldn't deliver, it hurt! It hurt me, Mommy. And no matter what you hoped for, I'll never be more than what I am. And you never see that: what I really am!"

June's mother stares at her, tears welling up in her eyes. Then she takes the chain off her neck and offers it to June, who refuses it. Her mother says in a pleading tone, "June, since your baby time, I wear this next to my heart. Now you wear next to yours. It will help you know, I see you. I see you."

June was not guilty of failing to meet self-imposed expectations. Yet, because she felt put upon, or shamed by her mother—rational or not—June also felt rejected by her. Of course, like it does with all of us, it only compounded her sense of shame.

Feelings of Emptiness

Anne Morrow Lindbergh, in her enchanting book *Gift from the Sea,* writes "When one is a stranger to oneself, then one is estranged from others, too. If one is out of touch with oneself, then one cannot touch others. . . . Only when one is connected to one's core is one connected to others."[6]

Shame cuts the core out of our being. Several authors have written on "the impostor phenomenon"—the belief that you do not deserve your success and that someday you will be exposed as a fraud. Often successful people have such a deep sense of shame that they put on masks to hide their hurt. Instead of shielding them, the masks only serve to make them feel like phonies.

Feelings of Loneliness

Shame robs people of the joy found in solitude, and it fills people with painful feelings of desperate aloneness. German theologian Paul Tillich said, "Language has created the word *loneliness* to express the pain of being alone, and the word *solitude* to express the glory of being alone."

For many people, loneliness is a serious personal problem, but because of shame, they do not have the strength they need to risk reaching out to people. They do not want to risk rejection, and so they withdraw. Even people who are socially active may keep their emotional distance to lessen the risk of rejection. As a result, they too suffer loneliness.

Feelings of Dependency

Thomas Merton said that the person "who fears to be alone will never be anything but lonely." The loneliness of shame fosters unhealthy dependency—what has been called "codependency." Instead of needing people in a healthy way—to love and be loved—shame-prone people need others to avoid being alone. They unwittingly become overly dependent in their relationships as an antidote for shame and from fear of rejection.

Shame-prone people will often feel inadequate, rejected, empty, lonely, and dependent. They may pity themselves, be passive, withdraw, and lose their creativity. All of these side effects are obviously cause for concern, but shame's greatest damage comes as a result of a single lie.

> *If you really do put a small value upon yourself, rest assured that the world will not raise your price.*
>
> ANONYMOUS

Shame's Looming Lie

The greatest lie lived by a shame-prone person is one that says, "I cannot change." Shame has a way of bullying people into a dead end with no exits. The shameful lie within them says, "I am what I am, and there is nothing I can do about it."

For his entire professional life, Martin Seligman at the University of Pennsylvania has been studying what makes people stop trying to change. As a twenty-one-year-old graduate student fresh out of college, he observed an experiment that set him on a quest for unraveling why some people give up while others overcome.

In the experiment, dogs were subjected to a minor shock, which they could avoid by jumping over a low wall that separated two sides of a shuttle box. Most dogs learned this task easily. But other dogs just lay down whimpering, with no will to try. When Martin investigated the dogs who had given up, he found that they had been used in a prior experiment in which they received shocks no matter what they did. These dogs had "learned" helplessness. Because they had been given shocks regardless of whether they struggled or jumped or barked or did nothing, they learned that nothing they did mattered. So why should they even try?[7]

Like the dogs in this experiment, people who are burdened with heavy doses of guilt and shame also have learned to be helpless. Because they believe that what they do makes no difference in what happens to them, they decide to give up.

During the Holocaust, many prisoners in the Nazi concentration camps also were in an apparently hopeless situation. But, as the psychiatrist Viktor Frankl observed, the prisoners who struggled to survive, who fought back against their captors, who refused to give up hope—those were the Jews who survived. But the Jews who gave up their will to live sickened and died quickly. In the same way, when we become victims of shame's looming lie, we lose all hope and falsely believe that living any other way is beyond our control.[8]

Many things in life are beyond our control—eye color, race, the earthquakes in southern California—but shame is not one of them. No one needs to live under the awful burden of shame. Instead, you can choose to change the way you think—especially the way you think about yourself.

Now that we have defined and diagnosed the problems of regret, guilt, and shame, the remainder of this book is dedicated to prescribing the real-life remedies for healing these deadly diseases of the soul.

For Reflection

1. Why do you think the emotion of shame is so toxic?

2. When have you experienced the emotional evolution of regret turning to guilt and guilt turning to shame?

3. If we typically feel guilty for things we've done and ashamed of who we are, what are the implications for healing from shame versus healing from guilt?

4. What does your score on the Shame Inventory in this chapter tell you about you and what you might need to do next?

5. The side effects of shame are often inadequacy, rejection, emptiness, loneliness, and dependency. What other emotional baggage does shame carry with it?

6. Once a person believes they cannot change because of "who they are," it becomes nearly impossible to see progress. When have you fallen victim to this paralyzing lie?

Part 3 | Living Without Regret

9

THE AMAZING ALTERNATIVE TO FEELING GUILTY

Sorrow is a sacred thing.

WILLIAM COWPER

Early Catholic guides for priests taking confessions warned about a type of person called "the scrupulous," people who held on to guilt no matter what. They were "unrelieved confessors" who, in spite of all assurances, could not accept grace.

If you are scrupulous, if you are holding on to your guilt like a security blanket, there is a better way. Not only can you know God's grace, but you can *experience* it. The way to rid yourself of real guilt is through the path of godly sorrow.

Long ago, Paul had to write a letter to the Corinthians chastening them for their sins. When they responded by repenting and changing their behavior, he wrote:

Even if I caused you sorrow by my letter, I do not regret it. . . .
I am happy, not because you were made sorry, but because

> your sorrow led you to repentance. For you became sorrow-
> ful as God intended and so were not harmed in any way by
> us. Godly sorrow brings repentance that leads to salvation
> and leaves no regret, but worldly sorrow [guilt] brings death.
>
> 2 CORINTHIANS 7:8–10

While guilt and sorrow are sometimes seen as the same emotional experience, they could not be further apart. Sorrow, unlike guilt, does not wallow in self-punishment and self-abasement. Instead, it is grounded in a deep concern for relationships and constructive change. Sorrow's focus, outlook, and, most important, its results are radically different from the focus, outlook, and results of the emotion of guilt. While sorrow results in positive, life-affirming changes, guilt results in the destruction of self and relationships.

In this chapter we take a close look at eight important distinctions between godly sorrow and guilt and roll up our sleeves and walk step-by-step through a proven plan for internalizing godly sorrow in our lives and making positive and lasting changes. We begin, however, with the differences between these two emotions.

1. Godly sorrow focuses on the other person.

Guilt is a selfish emotion. When people feel guilty, they focus on themselves exclusively. Their pains from guilt are so great that they cannot begin to acknowledge the pain of the people they have hurt.

Godly sorrow, in contrast, allows people to look beyond their own pain and enter the world of the person they have offended. For example, the prophet Nathan tricked David into identifying with his victim when he told the story of the rich man who stole the beloved lamb of a poor man. Enraged by the incident, David declared, "As surely as the Lord lives, the man who did this deserves to die! He must pay for that lamb four times over, because he did such a thing and had no pity" (2 Samuel 12:5–6 NIV).

But Nathan turned to David and said, "You are the man! . . . You struck down Uriah the Hittite with the sword and took his wife to be your own" (2 Samuel 12:7, 9 NIV).

For the first time David realized what he had done to his victim, Uriah. He did not focus on himself. He did not say, "I'm the king—I can do whatever I want." Nor did he blame Bathsheba for seducing him. Rather, he acknowledged his sin against Uriah, confessed it to God, and was forgiven (2 Samuel 12:1–24).

2. *Godly sorrow recognizes pain as a part of the healing process.*

When I worked as a medical psychologist in the burn unit of the University of Washington Medical Center, I observed burn patients endure inhuman pain all in the hope of healing. I watched them painfully exercise tender limbs with the guidance of a caring rehabilitation therapist because they accepted the fact that healing only comes through pain. However, I have also worked with burn patients who refused physical therapy. Their highest priority was not to heal, but to avoid pain—and their physical healing was deferred because of it.

The feelings of guilt and sorrow work much the same way. Sorrow looks beyond the pain of the moment to the greater goal of healing a broken relationship. It cares about making a wrong

> *Earth has no sorrow that heaven cannot heal.*
> THOMAS MOORE

right. Self-absorbed guilt, on the other hand, refuses to go through the pain required to heal a relationship.

3. *Godly sorrow looks forward to the future.*

Years ago a small town in Maine was proposed for the site of a great hydroelectric plant. Since a dam would be built across the river, the town itself would be submerged. However, out of fairness, the people were given several years to arrange their affairs and relocate.

Because of this decision, the town council canceled all improvements. No one repaired or painted buildings, roads, or sidewalks. Day by day the whole town got shabbier and shabbier. A long time before the flood waters came, the town looked uncared for and abandoned, even though the people had not yet moved away. As one citizen explained, "When there is no faith in the future, there is no power in the present."

On the one hand, people troubled by feelings of guilt do not care about or plan for the future. Obsessed with the history of their failures, they cry futilely over situations that cannot be changed. Instead of driving with their eyes on the road ahead of them, they continually look behind them. But with their eyes focused on the rearview mirror, they cannot drive straight—and so they cause yet another accident. Constructive sorrow, on the other hand, looks to the future. It keeps the eye trained on the road ahead, with only quick glances behind to prevent accidents.

In graduate school, I worked for a short time in a treatment center for senior adults. One of my patients, Madeline, was almost ninety. Her husband, a decorated major in the U.S. Air Force, had passed away three years before. Madeline's room at the center was filled with memorabilia. Travel souvenirs and photos of deceased friends decorated her walls and shelves. But on her ninetieth birthday, Madeline took down most of the mementos from her past and replaced them with pictures of places and things she wanted to learn about. "You might think I've gone crazy," she told us. "But I just want to start living again, and I've got to start thinking about my future."

Madeline turned her back on the sunset and smiled her welcome to the sunrise. Godly sorrow is the same way. It helps people turn their back on the past and start planning their future. Sorrow does not obsess over the way things might have been. It does not revel in regrets. Sorrow envisions what life can become and believes it will be better than the past.

4. Godly sorrow is motivated by our desire to change and grow.

People who are plagued by feelings of guilt will do anything to make themselves feel better. But often their attempts at change do not last long. As soon as they feel the burden of guilt lift, they are back to their old destructive patterns of behavior. Constructive sorrow, on the other hand, is motivated by our desire to make needed changes in our behavior and attitude.

I grew up in a church that sponsored old-fashioned revivals. For more than a week, an evangelist would come and preach every day, in the morning and in the evening. And normally, at the end of each service, people would come forward to the altar and repent of their sins. After a time, I noticed that often the same people would kneel at the altar in successive services.

Why would people need to confess their sins over and over again? The answer is simple. What do you want more than anything else when you are loaded with guilt? You look for a place to leave it. So, instead of changing the behavior that leads to your guilt, you go forward and "leave it at the altar."

> God whispers to us
> in our pleasures,
> speaks in our
> conscience, but
> shouts in our pains:
> it is his megaphone
> to rouse a deaf
> world.
>
> C. S. LEWIS

Released from your burden of guilt, you then fall back into your old patterns of behavior. Your "repentance" takes away your painful guilt, but it does not cure your problem.

Guilt brings us back to where we began in an endless cycle of bad behavior and shallow repentance. Godly sorrow, on the other hand, motivates us to make long-lasting changes that, although are painful, can break the cycle of guilt and sinful behavior.

5. *Godly sorrow is a choice; it is not coerced.*

God knows that a genuine confession is rarely coerced. Through friends, spouses, counselors, Scripture, or his Spirit, he gently leads us to a realization of our wrongdoings, then enables us to confess our sins and change our behavior.

Remember the story of the woman caught in adultery (John 8:2–11)? One morning, while Jesus was teaching in the courtyard of the temple, a group of Pharisees and teachers of the law burst in dragging a woman behind them. "Teacher, this woman was caught in the act of adultery!" they shouted. "The law says we are to stone such a woman. What do you say?"

There was deathly silence. Everyone waited to hear his answer. Jesus knew they were trying to trick him: If he said to stone her, he would be disobeying the Roman law, which forbade carrying out the death sentence. But if he told them not to stone her, he would be disobeying God's law. Jesus bent down and wrote in the sand. When the men continued to pester him, he said, "If any of you is without sin, throw the first stone!"

The angry mob fell silent and stole away, one by one. The trembling woman and Jesus were left standing together.

"Where are they? Has no one condemned you?" he asked her.

"No one."

Jesus brushed the dirt from his hands. "Then neither do I condemn you," he told her. "Go now, and leave your life of sin."

I've often wondered if Jesus made a mistake when he said that. I mean, shouldn't he have gotten her to promise to change *before* pronouncing his forgiveness? But that's not Jesus' way of responding to guilt. He did not want a coerced confession motivated by fear. He wanted her to *choose* a better way of living in order to *be* a better person.

6. Godly sorrow relies on God's mercy.

Often we tend to feel that we must earn God's favor. When Martin Luther was still a Catholic monk, he struggled with unbounded feelings of guilt. He meticulously observed all the requirements of his religious order and confessed his sins repeatedly. He was so obsessed with confessing even the minutest sins that his superior once chided him: "If you expect God to forgive you, come into confession with something to forgive!"

When we relate to God out of a guilty conscience, we try to earn our worth by being severely critical of ourselves.

*Have courage
for the great sorrows
of life and patience
for the small ones;
and when you
have laboriously
accomplished
your daily task,
go to sleep in peace.
God is awake.*

VICTOR HUGO

Rather than relying on God's mercy, we struggle to show God how good we are. A sense of inadequacy drives us to prove that we are deserving of God's forgiveness.

Godly sorrow, on the other hand, allows us to fully accept and experience God's forgiveness. When Martin Luther came across Romans 1:17, "the righteous will live by faith," he saw the futility of all his good works. For the first time, he recognized the uselessness of trying to earn God's acceptance and rested in the gift of God's amazing grace. His decision to base his life on faith changed his life and revolutionized the church.

7. *Godly sorrow gives us a positive attitude.*

As a college freshman, I took a two-week wilderness expedition in the Coast Mountains of British Columbia. My guide, a man named Fraiser, was a sturdy man with a beard and wire-rimmed glasses who was at least fifteen years older than I. Looking at him, I thought I wouldn't have any trouble keeping up. After all, I was a cocky college student.

After a mere three days on my mountain journey, however, my hip bones were rubbed raw from the padded belt on my thirty-pound backpack. My feet were covered with open blisters, and my legs were as stiff as tent poles. I could hardly climb another step while Fraiser, whose pack was twice the size of mine, whistled a happy tune as he all but skipped up the path.

"I don't understand it," I finally blurted out. "I'm no slouch. How can you do this so easily while every step I take hurts from the waist down?"

Smiling, Fraiser handed me his canteen. "Because you approach this mountain the same way you approach college. You see it as a test. You have made the mountain your enemy and have set out to defeat it. Naturally, the mountain fights back. By the way it looks, it's winning!"

He laughed and continued walking. Only a few steps later I found myself whistling with Fraiser. The blisters still hurt, but I was gradually beginning to enjoy the journey. With each step higher, I felt the sun warming my head and the thin mountain air filling my lungs. I was seeing trees and breathing deeply the scent of pine needles. I began to look at the mountain as a friend, not as an enemy. As a friend, the mountain lifted me and carried me along.

When we feel guilty, we have a negative attitude toward ourselves. We work to control and defeat guilt, and as a result, the spiritual aches and pains thrive. But when we feel godly sorrow, we maintain respect for ourselves. We do not try to conquer the self as much as we try to empower it to continue the journey. Instead of becoming our own enemy, we treat ourselves with respect, as we would a beloved friend.

8. Godly sorrow results in real and lasting change.

Constructive sorrow results in a true life change while guilt, at best, spins us into a cycle of temporary change followed by more self-condemnation. I can almost hear some of you saying, "But feelings of guilt do motivate me to change my behavior." I agree. Guilt can lead to confession and change, but only in the short run. Motivation by guilt doesn't last. Life is a marathon, not a hundred-yard dash. Confession of guilt, in the absence of godly sorrow, short-circuits any attempt to make long-lasting life changes. The cycle looks like this:

Some entrepreneurs have turned this endless cycle of guilt feelings into a lucrative 900-number phone business. A soothing female voice comes on the line: "Have you ever done something you feel bad about? Call me at Phone Confessions to leave your own message. Tell someone how you feel or tell someone that you're sorry."

As many as 14,000 people call in every day to confess or apologize on this computerized phone line. Others simply call to listen to the recordings of confessions by other people. Callers pay two dollars for the first minute to eavesdrop on people baring their souls. Apparently, just listening to confessions, finding solace in the fact that there are others who feel bad about wrongdoings, helps some people deal with their guilty feelings. Not surprisingly, most of the money on this line is made from people who call repeatedly. In the same way, some people relate to God as if he were an automated confessional. They confess as a way to "get God off their backs," rather than as a means of empowerment for actual change in their behavior and attitude. In other words, confession for some is simply a means to feel better, not to become more healthy and whole.

Summary

Dr. Bruce Narramore, author of *No Condemnation,* provides several helpful handles in wrapping our minds around the distinctions of guilt and godly sorrow.[9] The following figure is adapted from Dr. Narramore's work and may help you understand the stark contrast between guilty feelings and godly sorrow.

	Guilty Feelings	**Godly Sorrow**
Focus	on one's self	on the person offended
Outlook	toward the past	toward the future
Motivation	to avoid painful feelings	to change and grow
Attitude toward God	I can do it alone	I need your help
Attitude toward self	frustration	respect
Result	temporary change or stagnation	progressive change that lasts

You Have a Choice

Gerald, twenty-six years old, came to see me about a persistent problem with depression. He told me that his struggle began when he was nineteen, about the same time he took his faith more seriously and became more active in his church. He told me about his regular times of sadness and self-pity. "God must hate me," he wailed. "I let him down all the time. I'm a failure and don't deserve his love."

After some gentle probing, Gerald broke down and confessed that his real struggle was sexual in nature. The weekend before he came to see me, he went on a date with a young woman from his church. After a movie and dinner, they drove to her apartment, and despite his determination not to get involved sexually, he couldn't resist her advances.

Gerald's "depression" did not originate in a chemical imbalance or from a grievous loss. His sadness was a mask for feelings of guilt that resulted from numerous, successive sexual encounters. "I've promised God I won't let myself get carried away like that," he said, "but I always end up failing him."

Gerald feels guilty, but he does not want to give up his sexual behavior. He carries a heavy burden of guilt, but it does not move him to be different. In fact, his guilt is what keeps him stuck. As long as he wallows in guilt, he is refusing God's grace, and his sexual trysts will remain a part of his life.

Gerald has all the signs of being entrenched in unhealthy guilt. His guilty feelings are doing nothing to help him change. His focus is self-centered, and he is obsessed with his past. He cares more about the pain he is feeling than about the pain he causes his women friends. He is trying to earn his worth rather than accepting God's grace. And above all, he has replaced his self-respect with frustration and anger.

Gerald does not yet realize he has a choice. He has determined that his guilt alarm is not false. But he is not aware of the choices he can make for the better. He can choose to focus on the future. He can choose to accept God's grace. And he can choose to make real and lasting changes in his behavior.

> *The slightest sorrow for sin is sufficient if it produces amendment.*
> C. C. COLTON

Every guilt alarm presents us with a choice. First, we decide if the warning is true or false. Next, if we know our feelings of guilt are the result of an act of wrongdoing, we are then faced with another decision. Will we choose to wallow in self-punishment by beating ourselves over the head with more guilt, or will we choose to experience constructive sorrow? Our options look like this:

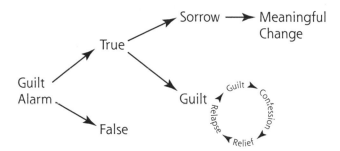

If you are in guilt's grip, choose the road less traveled—constructive sorrow and personal change. Follow these steps, and they will lead you on the way to godly sorrow:

1. Be honest.

When guilt is real, there is no escape. To rid yourself of real guilt, you must start by taking responsibility for your misdeeds. You must be honest about the hurt you have caused others as well as the pain you have caused yourself.

2. Focus on the person who has been wronged.

Look beyond your own pain to see if others are also hurting. Make a list of persons you have harmed or hurt. In Gerald's case, he had violated a relationship with his date and had broken a promise with God. All he can see, however, is his own pain. By lifting his vision beyond his self-centered feelings, he could take steps to repair the damage and promote genuine healing.

3. Confess your misdeed.

The very act of confession is a healing process. Sometimes, however, confession can be used as an excuse to wallow in guilt. Therefore, confession must be done with discretion. When your confession is likely to cause more pain than healing, confess to an objective person who knows how to keep a confidence. A pastor or a therapist, for example, might be helpful. In Gerald's case, he chose to confess to a counselor. But regardless of how you confess and talk about your guilt to another person, it is critical that you confess your misdeed to yourself and to God.

4. Ask for forgiveness.

Fulton Sheen, a popular Catholic priest in the fifties and sixties, said, "The only unforgivable sin is the denial of sin, because by its very nature, there is now nothing to be forgiven." If possible, and without causing further damage, ask forgiveness from whomever you have wronged. It may be a friend, a family member, or a coworker. It may be God, or even yourself. Regardless of who it is, you must ask forgiveness for what you have done wrong. Gerald, for example, needed to ask the woman he had wronged to forgive him.

5. Make it right.

Restitution is the old-fashioned word we explored earlier in this book, and as we consider godly sorrow it deserves to be revisited. You may recall that the dictionary defines *restitution* as "an act of restoring something to its rightful owner." As I noted in chapter 2, stealing in earlier times was usually related to tangibles such as hand tools or chickens. Restitution was far more straightforward then than it is today, because life is now more complicated. But while restitution may be complicated, it is an important step in finding freedom from real guilt. In Gerald's case, he could not do much to repair the harm he had done other than to ask for forgiveness from his date. You may recall that I called this "relational restitution." So, if you need to, take a look back in this book where I gave more tips for putting this valuable principle into practice (see p. 38).

6. Accept forgiveness.

Accepting forgiveness is often the most difficult step in healing guilt. The conscience doesn't want to give up its power. But you will not rid yourself of guilt until you take the final step of accepting forgiveness. Sometimes restitution is not possible. Sometimes the offended person refuses to forgive you. But that is her problem, not yours. If you are genuinely sorry, have honestly tried to make it right, and have sincerely asked God for forgiveness, you can be confident you are forgiven. "If we confess our sins, he is faithful and just and will forgive us our sins" (1 John 1:9). Because Gerald had a difficult time accepting God's forgiveness, his self-condemnation kept him mired in his sin. By accepting forgiveness, he could be free of the guilt that would drive him to sin again.

> *There is a sweet joy that comes to us through sorrow.*
> CHARLES HADDON SPURGEON

7. Look to the future.

Asked which of his works was his masterpiece, architect Frank Lloyd Wright, at the age of eighty-three, replied, "My next one." Envision in detail the design of a better future rather than mulling over your past failures. Gerald was so consumed with how "rotten" he was for what he had done, he hadn't taken the time to construct a future that looked any different from his past.

8. *Ask yourself why you want to change your behavior or attitude.*

Do you want to promote growth and improve your relationships, or do you merely want to avoid the painful feelings of guilt? Gerald didn't really want to behave differently. He simply wanted to feel better about himself without having to sacrifice his selfish desires.

9. *Rely on God's strength to help you overcome.*

Humbly admit you are powerless to overcome your guilt alone, and make a decision to turn your will and life over to the care of God. Gerald, for example, was trying to be the kind of person he wanted to be without depending on God's grace to help him change. Therefore, he repeatedly fell into the same sin.

10. *Respect who you are as a person.*

You can be deeply remorseful without surrendering your self-respect or dignity. Paul, who was "sorrowful, yet always rejoicing," understood this principle (2 Corinthians 6:10). Gerald admitted his wrongdoing but did so in defeat. In a state of helplessness, he was frustrated and angry with himself. In his scenario, there was no place for change.

In this chapter we have looked at how to handle feelings of true guilt effectively so as to diminish their pain and make real and lasting changes in our lives. In the next chapter we will examine the problem of false guilt, which can be as debilitating as real guilt, but whose cure requires a different approach.

For Reflection

1. When have you felt "scrupulous"—holding onto your guilt like a security blanket? Why did you do this?

2. When have you stepped beyond guilt by applying the gift of godly sorrow to your own situation?

3. How has godly sorrow enabled you to turn the focus away from yourself and toward other people?

4. How has godly sorrow enabled you to look forward to the future rather than to the past?

5. Have you ever experienced the cycle of guilt, confession, relief, and relapse or have you seen others go through it? How can you short-circuit this destructive cycle?

6. After you review the steps for experiencing godly sorrow outlined in this chapter, what will be your most difficult step? What can you do about it?

10

SAYING GOODBYE TO FALSE GUILT— FOREVER

From the body of one guilty deed
a thousand ghostly fears and haunting thoughts proceed.

WILLIAM WORDSWORTH

Knowing that her nine-year-old daughter, Nicole, was getting out of school at noon, Janice took a day off to run errands and spend time with Nicole. All morning she ran from place to place, shopping for groceries, picking up clothes at the dry cleaners, and depositing money at the bank. By noon she was home to greet Nicole and fix lunch. Then she and Nicole spent several hours baking a cake and planting bulbs in the garden. By 3:00 Janice was exhausted. She stretched out on the couch, intending to relax only for a moment, but she quickly fell asleep. When she woke up fifteen minutes later, she found her daughter watching television. Janice kicked herself. *Here I was going to make this a special day for Nicole, and I had to fall asleep! I'm a terrible mother,* she thought.

Janice, however, is *not* a terrible mother. She *had* fulfilled her intention of spending time with her daughter, and she obviously had needed a brief nap. But Janice, because of her overactive conscience, struggles with the problem of false guilt.

In the previous chapter I showed how to deal with *real* guilt through the pathway of godly sorrow. But what do we do with *false* guilt? Since false guilt is not caused by any real wrongdoing, godly sorrow does not eradicate it. In fact, false guilt does not deserve the same treatment as true guilt. To apply God's forgiveness to guilt that does not exist cheapens his gift of grace. We must therefore be careful to distinguish between real and false guilt and apply the remedy that best treats the sickness.

> *The purpose of being guilty is to bring us to Jesus. Once we are there, then its purpose is finished. If we continue to make ourselves guilty—to blame ourselves—then that is sin in itself.*
>
> CORRIE TEN BOOM

Although there are no fail-safe remedies to the disease of false guilt, I've found several steps you can take to ameliorate its pain and reduce the frequency of its attacks on your conscience. I don't want to bog you down with extraneous detail at this stage. Some of these steps will be reminiscent of what we have already talked about at greater depth (see chapter 5). I simply want to offer these steps for consideration as a kind of action-summary and ask that you, once again, think about them in relationship to the overarching goal you set for yourself at the beginning of this book.

1. Distinguish between real guilt and false guilt.

To review, real guilt is caused when we break the law—either the law of the land or God's moral law. False guilt, however, is not a result of breaking any laws. Rather, false guilt is a trap and a lie devised by Satan to keep us in bondage to negative feelings.

At the root of false guilt is the idea that what you *feel* must be true—or, in other words, if you *feel* guilty, you think you must have *done* something wrong. However, emotions can lie because they are not products of reality, but of our *interpretation* of reality. Distorted thoughts and beliefs give birth to emotional distortions.

If your guilt alarm won't stop sounding, ask yourself what objective evidence could be summoned to prove your fault. If you cannot find evidence of wrongdoing, you are suffering from false guilt, an emotion that is based on feeling, not fact.

2. Beware of expectations.

People suffer needless guilt when they put themselves at the mercy of their own expectations. In a sense, they are setting themselves up to fail by expecting more than they can possibly receive. Therefore, challenge your unspoken expectations in specific terms. For example, what do you expect at work? Do you think, *My boss will always recognize my good work and thank me for it?* What are your expectations at home? Do you think, *My family will praise me for how clean the house is,* or *They will recognize how hard I work to keep this home running on a predictable schedule?* What do you expect from your friends? Do you expect them never to let you down? What are your expectations about church? Do you expect everyone to be consistently loving and accepting?

Even posing these questions suggests their absurdity. Turn your expectations into wishes and even then, don't take them too seriously. If you want a little recognition for your hard work, then ask for it. Don't set yourself up to feel like a failure because someone hasn't responded in the way you deserve. Carefully examine your unrealistic expectations, for if they are unspoken, they may also be unrecognized.

Take a moment to write down the private expectations that unwittingly set you up for battles with false guilt. This simple exercise will help you reeducate your conscience so you can become more flexible with yourself.

3. *Say goodbye to perfectionism and hello to being human.*

When a person wants to comfort a friend who has made a mistake, he'll often say, "You're only human—you're supposed to make mistakes!" Guilt-prone people, however, think they should never make any mistakes. They have unrealistic goals, and they ignore human weakness.

Perfection is the ultimate illusion, for it simply does not exist on this earth. When people try to live under self-imposed perfectionist standards, they will forever be tormented by unnecessary guilt. Their guilt will make them feel inept, disappointed, and depressed. One of my students, for example, felt he brought disgrace to his family by not making all A's. That is unreasonable. No one can be perfect!

Of course, this does not mean we should not aim for high standards. There is a difference between perfectionism and excellence. Thomas Peters and Robert Waterman Jr., authors of the best-selling *In Search of Excellence,* describe excellence not as attaining an impossibly out-of-reach goal but as living up to your potential. Everyone has the potential to attain excellence in his or her life.

When you wake up each morning, give yourself permission to be wrong. Strive for excellence, but not perfection. And as a human, remember that you're *supposed* to make mistakes.

4. *Realize it is okay to say no.*

Are you able to say no to things you don't want to do and not feel guilty? Saying no to a request is not a sin. Some people believe that passive agreeableness is the same thing as virtue, decency, and honor. It is not. Passivity has more in common with wimpishness than civility or good manners. I have always had difficulty saying no to speaking invitations. Some time ago my "yeses" were doled out so easily that my speaking schedule began to interfere with other important responsibilities. One day a kind and trusted colleague took me to lunch. He asked me about my speaking schedule and after patiently listening said, "Les, you know it's okay to say no, don't you?" Somehow his words helped me to set better boundaries, and I began to learn to meet other people's needs without sacrificing my own.

Do you have difficulty saying no? Be honest. Ask yourself what you would do in these circumstances. A close friend asks you for a loan. Your least favorite aunt tells you she is coming to visit. A salesperson pressures you to buy his product. Your boss asks you to postpone your vacation. Your pastor asks you to teach the junior high Sunday school class for the next eight weeks.

It is okay to disagree and it is okay to say no. If you are having difficulty standing your ground because guilt urges you to give in, learn to be assertive. To start with, ask for more time before making a decision. Give yourself an opportunity to think about the implications of "a small favor" before you agree to do it.

Next, ask yourself, "What am I feeling?" The guilt-prone person is more likely to ask, "What *should* I be feeling?" But this question is irrelevant. Focus on how you *honestly* feel. Once you have identified your feelings, talk about them with a trusted friend and get his or her objective feedback. Your feelings are neither good nor bad; they are just your feelings. Talking them out will clarify your thinking and help you reach a healthy decision. If you decide it is better to say no to a pushy salesperson or an intrusive relative, say no! A no doesn't even require an explanation. You don't have to feel guilty for setting up boundaries to protect your own sense of well-being.

> *Therefore, there is now no condemnation for those who are in Christ Jesus.*
> ROMANS 8:1

5. Concentrate on being rather than doing.

Trying to *look* good is exhausting. It is less work and much more rewarding to focus instead on trying to *be* good. If false guilt is a hound at your heels, shift your focus from *doing* the right thing to *being* the right person.

God does not wait for us to do the right thing to accept us. In fact, Paul wrote, "But God demonstrates his own love for us in this: *While we were still sinners,* Christ died for us" (Romans 5:8, emphasis mine). God's love and acceptance of us is what enables us to love and be kind to others: "We love because he first loved us" (1 John 4:19).

Think about what you are like when you are with a close circle of friends who accept you in spite of your blemishes.

You are probably relaxed, happy, and loving. Now think about what you are like around a group that withholds their acceptance of you until you have measured up to their expectations. Hoping to do and say the right things, you probably walk around on eggshells.

When we focus on *doing* rather than *being,* we more than double our chances of suffering from false guilt.

6. If you are still stuck, get help.

One of my favorite comics is a drawing of a boy in distress yelling to his dog: "Lassie, get help!" In the next frame, Lassie is lying on a couch in a psychologist's office.

If you have battled false guilt with little success, I urge you to seek professional help. Once you speak about your struggles to someone you trust, relief is normally not far away. You will be able to view yourself from a freer, less tyrannical perspective.

You may also find great help in a small group. Please consider this. And if you can't find one, start one (a local church can help you get one going). Being with other people who are walking the same path as you has tremendous healing power. If you are nervous about coming out of hiding and bringing your struggles with regret, guilt, or shame into the open, into companionship with others, I understand. This is one of those tough decisions I mentioned early on in this book. But take comfort in the fact that you are not alone, and vulnerability begets vulnerability. You will garner more respect from others than you ever imagined when you are honest about your own struggles within the context of community.

Community, especially in a church setting that provides space for honest struggles, is transformative. There is no need for you to walk alone on this journey. The experience is too universal and the rewards of joining others is too great.

For Reflection

1. Think of an example in your own life where you felt guilty over something that didn't deserve this kind of self-punishment. What can you learn from your false guilt?

2. How could you get in touch with objective evidence when you are wallowing in feelings of guilt?

3. What expectations do you place on yourself that might be causing you to suffer needless guilt?

4. When was the last time you said no and did not experience a pang of guilt? What is keeping you from setting boundaries?

5. If you can't shake a case of false guilt, what might prevent you from seeking the help of a trusted counselor?

11

DARING TO FORGIVE
YOURSELF

> The pain we cause other people becomes
> the hate we feel for ourselves.
>
> LEWIS B. SMEDES

No one inspired me more as a communicator during my graduate school days than Lew Smedes. And no one wrote more eloquently of the art of forgiving than he. His book *Forgive and Forget* topped the best-seller list when it was released two decades ago, and it is still viewed as a ground-breaking work, opening up the floodgates for research and writing on this neglected topic. Nearly every book written on forgiveness since has acknowledged his seminal work.

Just six months ago I flew from Seattle to Los Angles to attend Lew's funeral. He was eighty-one. Four of his closest friends and colleagues each hailed him as the apostle of for-giveness. What made his message on this subject so mean-ingful, insightful, and practical? I believe it was because he never diverted his gaze from human pain. Lew's genius was that he never allowed his heart to stray from his mind. So when he wrote and spoke of forgiveness, I savored every word—especially in his classroom. Lew was not one to lecture from an academic podium. He walked between the chairs and asked questions right in your face, which called on every ounce of courage you had to answer by matching his boldness. Lew wasn't looking for pat answers. He was into the nitty-gritty issues of life—which is why I learned more from him than anyone else on daring to forgive yourself.

I tell you about my late friend Lew because it would be unfair not to. My thinking on forgiveness has been so shaped by his that it would be dishonest not to acknowledge it right from the start. I dedicate this chapter to him and to you—to all of us who are pilgrims forging a path toward a more grace-filled life. I begin by underscoring the profound courage self-forgiveness takes and then provide a self-test that will help you know where you are in this process. Next, I reveal the sign that self-forgiveness is necessary and, most important, explain exactly how you can go about forgiving yourself.

The Courage of Solitaire Forgiveness

We lie to ourselves. We blame ourselves. We condemn ourselves. So it only stands to reason that we, on occasion, need to forgive ourselves. Many would argue that, in fact, this kind of forgiveness requires the most bravery. For truth be told, we may conjure up forgiveness for others who have hurt us, but if we cannot find forgiveness for ourselves, we will forever live in a prison of our own making—too afraid to face the freedom that is ours for the taking.

Brooks Hatlen is a good example. *The Shawshank Redemption,* one of my favorite films, depicts Brooks as a man who has spent his prime wasting away in prison because of a reckless act of violence he committed as a teenager. After forty years of incarceration, Brooks finally receives his release to enjoy his much talked about freedom.

On the outside, however, Brooks discovers that he can't enjoy it at all. He's grown accustomed to life within the constraints of a prison where he didn't have to make his own decisions. Someone else did the thinking for him, and now, on the outside, he faced a prospect more daunting and terrifying than incarceration: freedom.

> *How unhappy is he who cannot forgive himself.*
> PUBLILIUS SYRUS

This newfound freedom scares Brooks so much so that he confesses to contemplating various ways of breaking his parole in order to return to the security of his prison cell. He sums up his dilemma in one line: "It is a terrible thing to live in fear."

And it is. Anyone who lives in fear of forgiving oneself knows exactly what Brooks meant. For once you forgive yourself, you are no longer constrained by self-condemnation. You are free from a punishing conscience that can no longer beat you down. But forgiving yourself is not an easy task. To make it so would reduce this brave act to mere excuse making. And, of course, it is not about avoiding blame. Forgiving yourself is about facing guilt and embracing the freedom that comes from rising above it. It is about making peace with the part of your self you wish you could disown. It is about becoming healthy and whole.

Are You Ready to Forgive Yourself?

Forgiveness is the healing balm of bruised relationships. Most marriages or friendships, for example, would shrivel up and die without a generous supply of forgiveness. The pain we cause each other is too plentiful. So, somewhere within our souls, we muster up the courage to forgive—and our relationships move forward. But this same act of forgiveness we give to those we love is in short supply when it comes to ourselves. And that may hurt our relationships more than we ever imagined. If we can't forgive ourselves, we carry a burden of guilt that is sure to keep us from effectively loving the people we cherish the most.

The following quiz will help you determine your forgiveness quotient, not for those around you, but for the person who matters most—you. There are no right or wrong answers. Read through each item thoughtfully and circle the letter that most closely represents you.

1. If a product were invented called "Guilt-Be-Gone" that promised to instantly erase your burden of shame and help you forgive yourself with just a few squirts, you would:

    A. Wonder why anyone would ever need a product to forgive themselves.

    B. Purchase a can or two to have on hand when needed.

    C. Buy a case load to use almost weekly.

2. At any given moment the words that most aptly describe your attitude toward yourself are:

    A. Grace and mercy.

    B. Love and insecurity.

    C. Guilt and shame.

3. Some say feelings of guilt are like a light that goes off on the dashboard of your car. If this were the case, what would you think if you saw the guilt light flashing:

    A. There is a short in the wiring.

    B. I should probably check that out.

    C. I'm in serious trouble and need an overhaul.

4. Which statement most accurately reflects your feelings?

    A. I hold my head high and can look in the mirror with a very clear conscience.

    B. When it comes to accepting myself, I have good days and bad days.

    C. I don't think I'll ever be able to forgive myself for some of the things I've done.

5. *Guilt* and *gold* come from the same origin, meaning "to pay." When we feel guilty, we often feel that we must "pay" for our misdeeds. So if you were balancing your emotional checkbook:

    A. You'd leave it to your accountant.

    B. You would write a few checks and move on.

    C. You would know who to pay, but feel like you'd never have enough to give them.

6. I can forgive most everyone else, but I don't think I'll ever be able to forgive myself.

    A. False.

    B. Sometimes true, sometimes false.

    C. True.

7. At dinner with a close friend, you say something you instantly regret but don't apologize. Later that night you:

   A. Think she'll get over it so you go to bed for a deep sleep. After all, these kinds of things happen between friends.

   B. You decide to phone her sometime tomorrow to apologize and, as a result of your decision, are able to enjoy a sound sleep.

   C. You send her a heart-felt apology by email but still stay up most of the night wrestling your conscience.

8. Think about your greatest regret in life. Perhaps it's a failed marriage. Maybe a moral faltering. Whatever it is, how are you coping?

   A. I take responsibility for my actions but decided to let it go and move forward.

   B. I regret it to this day and will probably carry it forever.

   C. I not only feel guilty for what I did, I feel ashamed of who I am.

9. Catholic priests are warned about "scrupulous" people who come to confessions but hold on to guilt no matter what. They are known as "unrelieved confessors" who, in spite of all assurances, cannot accept grace. Are you a "scrupulous" confessor?

   A. Definitely not. I don't even need to confess to clear my conscience.

   B. Yes and no. Confession sometimes make me feel better, but guilt has a way of finding me again.

   C. Definitely yes. Even after friends and family have assured me, I still feel like I'm caught in the guilt trap.

10. Forgiving myself:

   A. Allows me to put the past behind me and move on.

   B. Is a struggle but I'm getting better at it.

   C. Is nearly impossible for me.

Scoring

Add up the number of A's, B's, and C's you have. Then check your answers below.

Mostly A's

It is safe to say that you are not wracked with guilt. Nobody ever accused you of having an overactive conscience. While you may have a few regrets, you are not the kind to linger on them. You keep moving forward and allow the past to stay behind you. And while you may not need help in learning to forgive yourself, we have a few suggestions to keep you healthy:

- Be sensitive to the sensitive. Truth be told, you are probably irritated by people who clobber themselves with guilt. "You're just a guilt monger," you may be tempted to say to a friend. But bite your tongue and simply listen. Without this sensitivity you may lose some relationships of great value.
- Guard against overcontrol. Because your guilt meter is relatively low, you run the risk of becoming hard nosed in your daily dealings—especially around the guilt prone. Instead of telling a colleague where you want to eat lunch, invite her to make suggestions and take them seriously.
- Don't neglect your conscience. While your ability to give yourself grace is an asset, you may need to guard against being too free with self-forgiveness. If you hurt your husband's feelings, for example, don't blow it off. Listen to your conscience and apologize.

Mostly B's

You walk a fine line between forgiving yourself and feeling guilty. Not that you are necessarily ambivalent, its just that you sometimes struggle to give yourself the grace you know you should. In a sense, you feel guilty about feeling guilty. So here's some tips to help you enjoy a deeper sense of peace more consistently:

- Recognize that your conscience is home-grown. Everyone feels guilty about different things, because we *learned* what to feel guilty about. If you feel guilty for not cleaning the kitchen before you go to bed, for example, it is probably because your mom did that. So evaluate your conscience and determine what you value (this will keep you from feeling false guilt).
- Practice saying no. This sounds silly, but if you will learn to say no without feeling guilty, you'll feel better about yourself. So the next time a friend asks for a ride that will cause you to be late to your daughter's recital, say no without regret or guilt.
- Ask for input. Chances are you don't hold others to a standard that is as high as the one you hold for yourself. As you sometimes struggle to forgive yourself, ask a trusted friend to give you feedback. "Is this something I should feel guilty about?" you may ask. Your friend's input can give you perspective.

Mostly C's

You are caught in a guilt trap that keeps forgiveness at an arm's length. While you may often forgive others, you can't seem to offer yourself the same grace. In spite of persuasion from friends and family, as well as evidence to the contrary, you still struggle with guilt and it's wreaking havoc on your relationships, not to mention your soul. You need to learn the rudiments of forgiving yourself and here are a few suggestions to get you started:

- Know the difference between true and false guilt. If you run a red light, you're guilty of breaking the law. But if you feel guilty for *thinking* about running a red light, you are *feeling* guilty without need. Feelings do not equal fact. Just because your guilt alarm goes off does not mean you *are* guilty.

- Focus on the majors. Some people caught in the guilt trap become "trigger-happy" confessors—to the point that asking for forgiveness loses it's meaning. "Can you forgive me for phoning during your dinner last night?" This minor offense (and millions like it) requires only an "I'm sorry," not forgiveness.
- Seek the help you need. If your nagging conscience is relentless, if you feel guilty to the point of depression, you need the objective help of a counselor. Call your physician for a referral. Sometimes a session or two is all it takes to put the past behind you and enjoy a deep sense of peace.

When Is Forgiving Ourselves Needed?

Many years ago I heard Norman Vincent Peale preach a sermon I have never forgotten. He tells the story of walking through the twisted little streets of Kowloon in Hong Kong, where he came upon a tattoo parlor. Peale was looking through the window at all the samples of available tattoos: an anchor, a flag, a mermaid, and many others. But he was surprised to see three words that could be tattooed on one's flesh, "Born to lose."

Peale entered the shop in astonishment and, pointing to those words, asked the Chinese tattoo artist, "Does anyone really have that terrible phrase, 'Born to lose,' tattooed on his body?"

He replied, "Yes, sometimes."

"But," Peale said, "I just can't believe that anyone in his right mind would do that."

The Chinese man simply tapped his forehead and said in broken English, "Before tattoo on body, tattoo on mind."

The tattoo artist knew exactly what was going on for the person who was weighed down by regret that had turned to guilt and guilt that had turned to shame. Self-inflicted condemnation is a tattoo on the mind of anyone who repeatedly blames herself and believes she is "worthless" because of some frailty, some mistake.

Let me say it straight: When you admit you have done something dreadfully wrong, something you did not have to do—and you wish to God you had not done it—you are blaming yourself. And when you blame yourself, you are ready to forgive yourself.

How to Forgive Yourself

The University of Michigan Institute for Social Research studied forgiveness in the lives of 1,423 adults and found that just over half (52 percent) have forgiven others for past transgressions. Three-quarters believe they have been forgiven by God for their mistakes. Forty-three percent have gone to others to be forgiven. Sixty percent say they have forgiven themselves at some point.[10] I don't know about you, but I'm struck by the fact that forty percent of us have never forgiven ourselves. We can learn a lesson from those who have. The question is, how did they do it. How does anyone forgive oneself?

It begins when we dare to do something that may seem silly at first but will soon seem profound. We need to make a pronouncement of our self-forgiveness out loud. Not to anyone else. Just to ourselves. We need to look squarely into the mirror and give ourselves absolution: "God forgives you and so do I." We need to meet our own eyes in the mirror and say it again. Of course, this statement won't instantly cleanse you from your condemnation, but it provides the beginnings for relief. It is a proven method for starting to clean the toxins of regret, guilt, and shame from your system. So look in the mirror and say it again. And again. Say it dozens of times—until you feel your heavy burden beginning to ease. And say a prayer of thanksgiving as God's grace begins to do its amazing work.

By the way, if you are having a tough time believing God forgives you—which is the foundation of self-forgiveness—remember that it is his idea. God invented forgiveness as a remedy for a past that not even he could change and not even he could forget. I want you to also remember something Charles Stanley said: "There is a loving heavenly Father who will forgive you of all of your sins, no matter what you've done, or how long you've done it." Keep that thought in mind as you remind yourself again and again that since God forgives you, you can forgive yourself too.

As you become more accustomed to receiving this spoken gift of forgiveness, it is imperative that you remain specific about what you are being forgiven for. In fact, the success of your self-forgiving is directly related to the concreteness of your wrongdoing. When we try to forgive ourselves in general categories, for "being mean" or "stingy," for example, forgiveness is deprived of the soil it needs to take root. Thus, we must name exactly what we need to forgive ourselves for: lashing out repeatedly at our child, being unfaithful to our spouse, and so on. This keeps us from being overloaded with undifferentiated guilt. It is best to forgive one thing at a time.

Keep in mind, by the way, that you may not always know when you have forgiven yourself. It is often an elongated experience, like hiking up switchbacks that take you higher but you can't really gauge your progress—not until you reach the top and survey the landscape you've traveled. And how do you know when you have reached the top, your destination, with forgiveness? You know it when you love freely. That's the sign. "She loves much because she has been forgiven much." That's what Jesus said to guests at a dinner in explaining why an uninvited woman would crash the party to wash his feet with expensive oils. Jesus understood that she had been forgiven much—and therefore loved extravagantly.

> *He who is devoid of the power to forgive is devoid of the power to love. There is some good in the worst of us and some evil in the best of us.*
>
> MARTIN LUTHER KING JR.

So the final step in self-forgiveness requires the confirmation of reckless love. It requires the free-flow of self-giving love. As Lew Smedes said, "How can you know for sure that you gambled with guilt and won unless you gamble your winnings on love?"

If you want to live as a person of forgiveness, do the sorts of loving things that forgiven people do. Write a letter of deep appreciation to your dad. Send a thoughtful gift to a person who jolted you. Reach out to someone who is lonely. Volunteer at a soup kitchen. Anything that stirs your self-giving spirit will bolster your self-forgiveness. In other words, a free act of love, to your unforgiving victim or anyone at all, is a sure sign that forgiveness has done and continues to do its work. It signals that you are both a forgiver and forgiven.

So there you have it: a few pointers on detoxifying your soul through self-forgiveness. I have deliberately added this chapter because if you are like most of us, fumbling and stumbling on our way to grace, you will need to be reminded of these principles. More than likely, your conscience will someday try to beat you up again. And when you hear the internal judge and jury pronouncing your guilt, you will need to remember that you are not doomed to serve the sentence. You will need to remember how to pull off this daring act of embracing your freedom once more. It's only human, but quite divine.

For Reflection and Discussion

1. Do you agree that self-forgiveness takes courage? Why or why not?

2. If your self-condemning statements were tattooed on your mind, what exactly would they say?

3. How do you feel about the suggestion of saying your message of forgiveness in the mirror? What might keep you from doing this and what will help you get past it?

4. Do you agree that the person who has been forgiven much loves much? How is this principle evident in your life?

12

YOUR INSURANCE POLICY AGAINST REGRET

This is our work in creation: to decide.

STEPHEN R. LAWHEAD

I'm on airplanes a lot. My speaking schedule keeps me criss-crossing this country almost weekly during certain seasons, which is why a recent news story about a US Airways flight from Philadelphia into my home city of Seattle caught my attention. On board was an unusual passenger—a pig.

Two passengers convinced the airline representative that the pig needed to fly with them as a "therapeutic companion pet"—like a seeing-eye dog—so the representative decided to permit the pig to sit with them in the first-class cabin of the plane. It was a decision he would soon regret.

Passengers described the 300-pound pig as "enormous, brown, angry, and honking." He was seated in three seats near the front of the plane, but the attendants reportedly had difficulty strapping him in: "He became restless after takeoff and sauntered through the cabin," one passenger said. "He kept rubbing his nose on people's legs trying to get them to give him food and stroke him."

Upon landing, things only got worse. The pig panicked, running up and down through economy class and squealing. Many passengers, also screaming, stood on their seats.

It took four attendants to escort the beast off the plane. And when they reached the terminal, the pig escaped only to be recaptured in another part of the airport.

When asked to comment on the story, US Airways spokesman David Castelveter said, "We can confirm that the pig traveled, and we can confirm that it will never happen again."

Ever felt like that? Who hasn't? You may not have allowed a 300-pound pig on board a passenger airplane, but you have probably made a decision about something and later said, "That will never happen again."

Poor decisions are at the root of every regret we experience. Every day at every turn we are making decisions, big and small, that determine our destiny. In the first chapter of this book, I posed an important question: At the end of your life, will you look back over time and be content with how you spent your days or will you wrestle with regrets? Of course, we all want to survey our days, our months, our years and view a life well lived. We all want a meaningful life of calm contentment. And the best predictor of being able to achieve it is how we make decisions.

> *Good plans shape good decisions. That's why good planning helps to make elusive dreams come true.*
> LESTER R. BITTEL

Decisions determine our destiny. So it only stands to reason that the best way to minimize your regrets—the surest insurance policy against them—is to learn how to make good decisions. Solid decisions. Quality decisions. The kind of decisions that, once made, allow us to never look back. And that's what this chapter is devoted to doing.

We'll begin with a reminder on the value of making decisions today that pay big dividends in the future. I'll then point you toward three "easy" decisions that, if not made in advance, become difficult. I then present a blueprint for making all difficult decisions easier. And I'll wrap up the chapter with a look at the single most important decision you will ever make, every day for the rest of your life.

Timing Is Everything

Some years ago in Chicago, I heard the renowned preacher Howard Hendricks give a powerful sermon entitled "The Message of Mistakes." In it he told the story of a wealthy man in his community that had the dubious distinction of having raised four children who couldn't have turned out more miserably: one in prostitution, two in drugs, and the fourth had been missing for the last ten years. Howard told how the man sat across from his desk one day and said, "Hendricks, I put my money on a dead horse." Howard then pondered what would happen if he were to say to the man, "Sir, I will guarantee to get your four children back if you'll do one thing."

"What is it?" the man would reply.

"If you will cut off your right arm," Howard would pose, "I'll guarantee to get your four kids back."

"Give me the knife," he'd answer. Then Dr. Hendricks paused and looked at the congregation and said, "This man would have no problem making the decision now, you see, but it's very late."

How true. As a psychologist, I've met plenty of moms and dads and husbands and wives who, now knowing how things have turned out, would give nearly anything to go back in time and do things differently. But it's wishful thinking. The best decisions we ever make are on the front end of a story, not at the conclusion. That's why as we explore the art of making good decisions, I want to be sure you consider what decisions you need to be making today that will impact your life tomorrow. In other words, what decisions should you be weighing right now that will determine how you will feel in a decade? If you are to look back over your life and be content, this question is critical. And it is one I have been pondering intensely these days.

It is our choices . . . that show what we truly are, far more than our abilities.

J. K. ROWLING

As I write these words, my wife, Leslie, and I are expecting our second child, a boy, to arrive in a few weeks. This little one will join his older brother. I can't begin to tell you how much time I, along with my wife, have put into thinking about the lives of these two children. Perhaps some might think I'm jumping the gun, after all, one of them is not even born. I disagree. I know I only have one shot at being a dad, and I don't want to wake up some day when they are teenagers or when they are young men and say, "If only I would have been a different kind of father. If only I would have spent more time with them."

Without a doubt, this would be one of the greatest regrets I can imagine, and I'm not about to let it happen. That's why

I'm making decisions on the front end that will impact our family twenty years from now. I know I could easily be consumed by my work, for example, but I want my lifestyle to speak volumes to these boys about how much they are loved. It would be easy to be carefree about what I do and how I spend my money, but I know my modeling will determine, in great part, their character. I know that how I treat their mother will have a lot to do with my boys' attitudes toward women. The choices I make about my religion and God will surely shape their souls. I have a dream, a vision, for the kind of men these little boys will become, and I know I don't get a second chance at being their father. So I'm making decisions now that will minimize my regrets in the future.

And I'm guessing you're doing the same thing. It may not be about parenting, but you have a dream. You have a vision for what you are going to invest your life in with the years you have on this earth. You have a dream for what matters most to you, and that dream entails being able to look back upon your life and say, "That was well done." So at the outset of this chapter, let me remind you that timing is everything when it comes to achieving a life well lived. The good decisions you make today minimize the regrets you will experience in the years to come.

Three Decisions That Are Always Right

In 1999 State Farm Insurance rated the most dangerous intersections for accidents in the United States. The winner, or more accurately, the loser, was the corner of Belt Line Road and Midway Road in Addison, Texas. There were 263 reported crashes at this intersection in the affluent Dallas suburb. That averages out to five wrecks each week and does not count numerous unreported fender benders.

Now I don't know about you, but with this bit of information, if I lived in Dallas, I can assure you I'd have an easy decision to make. I'd decide that I would drive out of my way to avoid the intersection of Belt Line and Midway. In my opinion, that's a no-brainer. And it got me thinking about other decisions that are just as easy. In fact, I want to pass along to you three decisions that should be easy, because they are almost always right, but have become too difficult for too many. So the next time you find yourself at a crossroads in any of these three areas, you will already know what direction to head.

Decide to Apologize When You're Wrong

"I'm sorry." When was the last time you uttered these two words? More important, when was the last time you knew you needed to and didn't? One of the easiest decisions you should ever make is to apologize when you are wrong. Why? Because saying "I'm sorry" has the power to repair harm, mend relationships, soothe wounds, and heal broken hearts. An apology has the ability to disarm others of their anger and to prevent further misunderstandings. And an apology, without a doubt, diminishes regret. While an apology cannot undo harmful past actions, if done sincerely and effectively, it can undo the negative effects of those actions.

A fellow father recently told me that he found his four-year-old trying to give his two-year-old sister a drink of water from his cup. The little girl's clothes were soaked, and he scolded his son for his carelessness. Only later did it dawn on the dad that his son had simply been trying to share his water with his little sister. The boy was being generous. "I knew I needed to apologize," said the dad. And he did. "I'm so sorry," he told the boy. "I shouldn't have scolded you when you were being so nice to share." And that was that. A simple apology set the scenario straight and they all moved forward. No resentment. No regret.

Apologizing is relatively easy. But for some reason, we don't always do it when we know we should. Something about our psyche makes it tougher than it needs to be. We'd rather harbor the hurt, it seems, than to own up to our actions. I recently read of a company in China, The Gift Center, whose main purpose is to deliver apologies and attempt to facilitate reconciliation for their customers. The company's motto is "We Say Sorry for You." That may work in an eastern culture, but I know it would never fly in my home. And I doubt it would work in yours either. So let me give you a few tips on how to say "I'm sorry."

A good apology involves three R's:

1. Responsibility: I know I hurt your feelings.
2. Regret: I feel terrible that I hurt you.
3. Remedy: I won't do it again.

Unless all three of these elements are present, the other person will sense that something is missing in your apology and he or she will likely feel shortchanged. Apology experts also suggest that you keep your apologies brief.[11] When you apologize over and over, it seems disingenuous. And keep it honest. Everyone has a built-in radar detector for a fake apology. And finally, steer clear of excuses. When you try to explain your mistake, you detract from your sorrow.

So there you have it—one easy decision you can make in advance that will simplify your life the next time you wonder whether you should apologize or not.

Decide to Tell the Truth When Tempted Not To

Joy, a nursing student at the university where I teach, landed her first job at a local clinic where, on her first evening of work, a young mother came in with her eighteen-month-old baby. The child needed his final shot for a routine immunization. The new nurse gave the boy his shot and stepped out of the room to record the vaccination on the boy's chart. As she did so, Joy noticed the seal on the vial inside her lab coat was unbroken. Instantly, she realized she had given the boy the wrong vaccine. Joy had given him a shot from a different vial—a routine vaccination for children, but the boy had already completed that series of shots months earlier.

> *I am convinced that life is 10 percent what happens to me and 90 percent how I react to it.*
>
> CHUCK SWINDOLL

Joy gasped when she realized her mistake and went into shock, physically numbed by what she had done. A series of thoughts raced through her mind: *I can't tell the doctor, he'll think I'm incompetent. It won't hurt the child to be immunized twice for the same thing, will it? But he does need the right vaccine. What would his mother do? No one will ever know. But I will always know. And so will God.*

Meanwhile, the doctor began examining the boy while Joy paced nervously around the nurses' station. When the doctor came out of the room, Joy immediately confessed her mistake. She knew she could not live with such a secret. As it turned out, no harm was done and the boy received the correct immunization.

Joy's story is a good example of what should be an easy decision but often isn't—to tell the truth when we are tempted not to. This simple decision, when lived out as an abiding principle, lowers a person's guilt and regret quotient significantly. So decide in advance, make a decision today, that you will tell the truth even when you're tempted not to.

Decide to Give As Best You Can

Tim Forneris is a twenty-two-year-old computer analyst who works part time as a groundskeeper for the St. Louis Cardinals. He is the one who retrieved Mark McGwire's sixty-second home-run ball, and he became famous for turning the ball over to McGwire instead of holding on to it and selling it for an estimated $1 million. Although *Time* magazine columnist Daniel Kadlec called this "an honorable gesture," he used Forneris as an example of some poor personal-financial habits.[12] Among Kadlec's pointers were the need to sleep on decisions before you act on them, avoid herd thinking, and treat "found money" seriously. Not surprising, Forneris wrote back to the columnist. Here is his thoughtful explanation of his actions:

> First of all, according to Mr. Kadlec, my first sin was the "impulse" decision to give the ball back to Mr. McGwire immediately. But my decision was by no means made on an impulse. I had thought over what I would do if I got a home-run ball and discussed it with my family and friends. Also, I can assure you that I was not influenced by herd thinking. What did influence my actions was my family and my

background. I have always been taught to respect others and their accomplishments. I value all people's achievements, big and small. In my opinion, Mr. McGwire deserved not only the home-run record for his work but also this ball. Life is about more than just money. It is about family, friends, and the experiences you have with them. As for my third financial sin of "easy come, easy go," I believe some possessions are priceless. To put an economic value on Mr. McGwire's hard work and dedication is absurd. Being the person who received the ball was a great blessing to me. And being able to return it to Mr. McGwire was a real honor and thrill. I still would not trade that experience for a million dollars.[13]

Wow! Would you have done what Tim Forneris did? I'm not sure I would have, but his story serves as a reminder of how valuable the quality of generosity is when it comes from the heart. Whether it be how much I tip a hurried server in a restaurant or how much I give to a homeless shelter in my home town, I have decided that I'd like to err on the side of giving too much than too little. Mind you, I'm not talking about being unwise or foolish with finances; I'm talking about deciding in advance to be the kind of person that gives as well as receives. It can be a relatively easy decision that we too often complicate. So remember Tim Forneris and you'll remember that giving almost always slays the dragon of regret.

> *What we decide is woven into the thread of time and being forever. Choose wisely, then, but you must choose.*
> STEPHEN R. LAWHEAD

How to Make Good Decisions
and Never Look Back

If you are like most people who have taken an introductory biology course in high school or college, you have dissected the notorious frog. You have labeled his various parts and pieces in an effort to accurately identify its workings. In the same way, we can benefit from exploring the anatomy of a good decision. What factors make up a decision that allows a person to never look back? As I have probed the issue, I've come up with eight essential questions that are a part of every good decision.

Are You Tired?

Sage advise recommends that you never cut down a dead tree in the winter. Making an important decision when you are tired runs parallel to this. Depleted of energy, your vision becomes blurry and your mind becomes cloudy. I know a frazzled woman who decided to sell her car because she didn't like the headache of maintaining it. Its repairs seemed to be more trouble than it was worth. The only problem was she couldn't afford a new car and her hasty decision left her stranded—literally. So this should be your first filter on making a good decision. Explore it when you are rested, not when you're exhausted.

Have You Questioned Your Motives?

Troy, one of my best students at the university where I teach, submitted his application and was accepted into a top-tier graduate program. Troy was on track to earn his Ph.D. in psychology from an institution that would open up numerous doors of opportunity. Two months before the move date, he came into my office to tell me he wasn't going. "What happened?" I asked. Troy explained that his church needed a youth pastor, and while he had been filling in they asked him to join the staff permanently. I was taken aback. Being a youth minister is certainly worthy, but he was passing on an opportunity that comes to only a very small percentage of people. He spiritualized his answer, and told me how God had "really been working on him." Well, who can argue with that? But I did press Troy a bit and we uncovered some other motives. Three months ago, Troy had started dating the daughter of the pastor at this church. You get the picture. Turns out, Troy's reasons for staying in Seattle had little to do with ministry and a lot to do with romance. Okay, that's fine. What's not fine is that he was not being honest with himself or anyone else. Long story short, Troy ended up going to graduate school that autumn and learned to navigate a long distance relationship—all because he exposed his real motives and faced the facts.

Have you Explored Your Options?

Let's say you are questioning a job offer that came to you unexpectedly. It would be more or less a lateral move to a different town, but something about it catches your interest. You think, maybe it's time for a change. But why? Are you bored? Tired of your colleagues? Stuck in a rut? What is getting you to take a second look at a job that really does little for you? If it really is time for a move, your decision deserves strategy, not the first little opportunity. That's the easy way out that is bound to leave you restless. Instead, when an opportunity sparks something within you, broaden your horizons. Consider other options. Think creatively and explore what else might await you.

Have You Weighed the Pros and Cons?

It's advice you have heard before, but the old trick of drawing a vertical line down the center of a paper and listing the potential positives and negatives about an issue you are exploring is sure to clarify the issue. Enough said.

Have You Considered Your Competence?

Sometimes a decision can be determined by your qualifications or your limitations. Whether it be your training, your skill level, your geographical location, or your financial resources, every important decision needs to recognize limits. As an author, I often hear from people who say they want to write a book, and they ask me for advice. And I'm always more than happy to offer it. But as soon as I review a sample chapter, I can quickly tell whether the person has the true capability to find their voice and really write. I'm sure you experience the same thing in your career. If you are in sales, for example, you know in a matter of moments whether somebody has what it takes to close a deal. The point is, as you are exploring an important decision, you've got to be honest with yourself about your limitations. Not that dreaming big and striving for audacious goals is off limits. Not by a long shot. But your personal competence needs to be a factor.

Have You Sought Counsel?

This may be the most important part of making a good decision. When you are in the midst of the proverbial forest, you may miss the trees. Asking someone else for input from their vantage point can be priceless. Two years ago, Leslie and I were invited by the governor of Oklahoma to be deeply involved in an initiative to lower the divorce rate in that state. We were honored. But since neither of us has ever been involved in politics or government work, we needed a lot of advice before making our decision.

We made a list of twenty people, some we knew and some we didn't, but all of whom we respected. And we requested their input on whether we should take on this responsibility or not. That exercise was one of the best things we could have done in making our decision. We eventually said yes to the invitation, but we did so not out of an initial impulse but rather from a studied perspective that involved some of the brightest minds we know. The point is that objective counsel is integral to making good decisions. If you are weighing a decision about your marriage, your family, your career, or anything else, it deserves the best advice you can get. So ask. Most people, even if you don't know them personally, are honored to give you counsel. Making a good decision is not a place to exercise rugged individualism. Proverbs says it plainly: "Plans fail for lack of counsel, but with many advisers they succeed" (15:22 NIV).

Have You Bathed the Process in Prayer?

Perhaps it goes without saying, but prayer is too important to take for granted. The author of James wrote, "If any of you lacks wisdom, you should ask God, who gives generously to all without finding fault, and it will be given to you" (James 1:5–6). God wants to guide us in our decisions. Psalm 32:8 says, "I will instruct you and teach you in the way you should go" (NIV). God often does this through prayer. So as you make decisions, don't neglect this valuable resource. And remember that prayer is a conversation. It is as much about listening as it is about asking.

Have You Decided to Make Your Decision a Good One?

This may sound silly at first, but every good decision involves another. Every good decision, in other words, is followed up by a decision to make that decision work. Let me explain. When I was about ten years old, my family made a huge move. Dad left his job in Portland, Oregon, and we traveled across the country by car to Boston where Dad would take on the new assignment as president of a college. It was a decision we made together as a family. And it was a decision that changed everything. New friends. New culture. New schools. The works.

> *The best decision-makers are those who are willing to suffer the most over their decisions but still retain their ability to be decisive.*
> M. SCOTT PECK

As we drove our car out of our driveway for the last time in Portland and passed familiar landmarks, the mood was solemn. Nobody spoke but you could feel the sadness of saying goodbye to a place we loved, and you could feel the anxiety of not knowing if this decision was a good one. When we drove east on Interstate 84 and got to the city limits of Portland, Dad pulled the car over to the side of the road. "Okay, folks," he said. "This is it. When we cross this line, we are leaving Portland behind us and starting a new chapter of our lives.

From here on we can decide to make this a good decision. But if we second guess ourselves and whine about how things are in Boston, we will forever regret it. So let's make up our minds right now to make this one of the best decisions this family has ever made." And we did. Dad's little pep talk taught me a lesson that day: to always decide that my decisions are good ones.

The Most Important Decision You'll Ever Make

If I did not convey what I am about to tell you at the close of this chapter on making good decisions, I would live to regret it. Truthfully. I feel compelled to, at the very least, mention the most important decision you will ever make.

It has nothing to do with your career path, your education, who you marry, where you live, what church to attend, or any of those significant decisions. No, this one is more important by far. For this decision drills down to the very heart of your happiness. It is a decision that, more than any other, determines the quality of your destiny.

> *The last of the human freedoms is to choose one's attitudes.*
> VIKTOR FRANKL

Consider the facts. Some people who have hit tough times still live radiant, happy, and productive lives. Others who have seemingly the same resources are beaten down, defeated, and riddled with regret. The first live in the present, the latter in the past. The reason for the discrepancy is not luck. The difference is attitude.

Some people who have every right to complain about what life has handed them decide to rise above their difficulties and live life to the fullest while others seem to almost roll over and give up, not knowing they have a choice. They don't realize that, as Abraham Lincoln put it, they are "about as happy as they make up their minds to be."

Perhaps you have heard the story about the devil having a yard sale. All his used tools were spread out and marked with different prices. He offered a fiendish selection. Hatred, jealousy, deceit, lying, pride—all of these were expensive. But a tool on display at the side of the yard was obviously more worn than any other tools. Surprisingly, it was also the most costly. It was labeled "discouragement."

When questioned about its high price, the devil said, "It's more useful to me than any other tool. When I can't bring down my victims with any of the other tools, I use discouragement, because so few people realize it belongs to me."

A little discouragement and a little regret from time to time is normal. But when the devil uses it to get a foothold in our spirits, it becomes a way of life that is sure to keep us down.

That's why the most important decision you'll ever make is to allow God to permeate your spirit. When you choose to accept his unconditional love, his transforming grace, your shackled soul sheds its weight and takes flight. Optimism and hope infuse your spirit as you rise above life's difficulties and choose the attitude that will steer your future.

Maya Angelou said, "If you don't like something, change it. If you can't change it, change your attitude." I couldn't agree more. It's the most important decision you'll ever make.

For Reflection

1. What is the best decision you ever made, and what went into your decision making process?

2. What is the worst decision you ever made, and what have you learned from that experience that has impacted how you make decisions today?

3. When it comes to moral decisions like telling the truth, what can you do now that will make those decisions easier?

4. How have you applied the most important decision you'll ever make to your own life?

NOW IS THE TIME

The future is not something we enter.
The future is something we create.
LEONARD SWEET

Cliff Satterthwaite sees himself as the priest at the altar of the past year. His New Year's Eve job is to help people cleanse their souls of regret of the past 365 days. Each year Mr. Satterthwaite sets up a booth in Fredericksburg, Virginia, where New Year's revelers come for a moment of solemnity. They write their regrets on a scrap of paper, then turn them to ashes in an adjacent canister. Literally, their regrets go up in smoke—or so the thinking goes.

By now you know that shedding yourself of regret is not necessarily that simple. Regret, when it lingers too long, becomes guilt. And guilt, in its petrified form, becomes shame. And shame is the most toxic emotion the soul ever encounters. So it stands to reason that when we overcome our regrets, when we learn what we can from what shoulda, coulda, or woulda been and move forward, we are doing holy work. When we step beyond the shadows of our past to become the person God intended, we are doing the most noble of human deeds. We are fulfilling our destiny.

So in this final chapter, I am going to make it short and sweet. No more need for tips and to-dos. No more need for exercises, self-tests, and steps. There's no more need to draw this out. I want the few words of this chapter to serve as a symbol for what must happen next. No more theorizing. No more explaining. Now is the time to make a choice.

I leave you with a story of a mythical golf match set in the 1930s in Savannah, Georgia, involving golf legends Bobby Jones, Walter Hagen, and hometown ace Rannulph Junuh. You may know the story as *The Legend of Bagger Vance*.

As a teenager, Junuh had tremendous promise as a golfer. But after his World War I tour of duty, he is marred psychologically and loses interest in golf. Content to gamble and drink, Junuh is a recluse until his former girlfriend invites him to join Jones and Hagen in an exhibition match. During the exhibition match, with four holes to play in the final round, Junuh successfully overcame his deficit of several strokes and took a two-stroke lead. But by the sixteenth hole, he trails again. On the seventeenth hole, he slices his tee shot deep into the woods. As he enters the dark forest to find his ball, panic overtakes him. The steam evaporating from the ground triggers memories of smoking battlefields where he watched all his company die. His hands tremble and he drops his clubs. Upon finding his ball, he calls it quits. He remembers why he quit playing golf and started drinking. Just then, Bagger, his golfing mentor, finds him and asks which club he'd like from his bag. He proceeds to tell Junuh that his problems have to do with the grip the past holds on him.

"Ain't a soul on this entire earth got a burden to carry he can't understand," Bagger consoles. "You ain't alone in that. But, you've been carrying this one long enough. It's time to lay it down."

Junuh admits, "I don't know how!"

Bagger replies, "You got a choice. You can stop, or you can start walking right back to where you've been and just stand there. It's time for you to come out of the shadows, Junuh! It's time for you to choose!"

"I can't," Junuh protests.

"Yes, you can," Bagger counters. "You're not alone. I'm right here with you. I've been here all along. Now play the game. Your game. The only one you were meant to play. The one that was given to you when you came into this world. Now's the time!"

And now is your time. Your past has held a grip on you for too long. You've been carrying regrets and guilt long enough. It is time to lay them down. On the pages of this book, I've done my best to show you exactly how to do just that. Like Junuh, you now have a choice. You can hold on to your guilt and regret or you can come out of the shadows of your past and fulfill your destiny.

It's your choice. I just have a couple quick reminders. First, you are not alone. God walks with you, giving grace at every step. And second, the tragedy of life is not that it ends so soon, but that we wait so long to begin it. Don't waste another day reliving what coulda been.

Now is the time.

NOTES

1. A. E. Mallinger and J. DeWyze, *Too Perfect* (New York: Random House, 1993).
2. A. W. Sussex "The Cost of Perfection," *Psychology Today,* January 2000.
3. M. Basco, *Never Good Enough: Freeing Yourself from the Chains of Perfectionism* (New York: The Free Press, 1999).
4. K. Norris, *Amazing Grace: A Vocabulary of Faith* (New York: Riverhead Books, 1999).
5. W. Hugh Missildine, *Your Inner Child of the Past* (New York: Simon and Schuster, 1971).
6. Anne Morrow Lindbergh, *Gift from the Sea* (New York: Pantheon, 1975).
7. Martin E. P. Seligman, *Helplessness: On Depression, Development, and Death* (San Francisco: Freeman, 1975). See also S. F. Maier and Martin E. P. Seligman, "Learned Helplessness: Theory and Evidence," *Journal of Experimental Psychology: General* 105 (1976): 3–46.
8. Viktor E. Frankl, *Man's Search for Meaning* (Boston: Beacon Press, 1962), 75.
9. Bruce Narramore, *No Condemnation* (Grand Rapids: Zondervan, 1984).
10. Information taken from chart in *USA Today,* 12 December 2001.
11. Beverly Engel, *The Power of Apology* (New York: John Wiley and Sons, 2001).
12. Daniel Kadlec, "Personal Time: Your Money," *Time*, 8 February 1999.
13. Ibid.

The Love List

*Eight Little Things
That Make a Big Difference
in Your Marriage*

Drs. Les & Leslie Parrott

This little book will make a big impact on your marriage. Start right away applying its hands-on concepts. You'll immediately increase intimacy, gain new direction, enjoy more laughter, and much more.

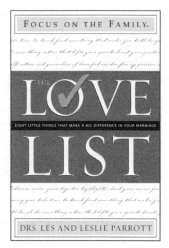

You'll love how *The Love List* unites purposefulness and spontaneity. "A few small actions—practiced on a daily, weekly, monthly, and yearly basis—can change everything for a couple," say relationship experts Les and Leslie Parrott. "Little, deliberate behaviors quietly lavish love on a marriage."

Drawing on their professional insights into successful couples and sharing candidly from their own marriage, the Parrotts give you eight simple-but-powerful, instantly usable principles that will lift your marriage out of the doldrums into everything you've wanted it to be. Plus, it's also fun! Especially when you start seeing noticeable results right away.

Hardcover: 0-310-24850-7

Pick up a copy today at your favorite bookstore!

ZONDERVAN™

GRAND RAPIDS, MICHIGAN 49530 USA

WWW.ZONDERVAN.COM

When Bad Things Happen to Good Marriages

How to Stay Together When Life Pulls You Apart

Drs. Les & Leslie Parrott

No matter how good your marriage is, it's not invulnerable. Bad things happen to the best of marriages. The question isn't whether you'll face struggles as a couple, but how you'll handle them when they come. When the going gets tough, what does it take to preserve—and in the long run, even strengthen—your union?

Relationship experts and award-winning authors Les and Leslie Parrott believe the same forces that can destroy a marriage can become the catalyst for new relational depth and richness—provided you make wise choices. You can even survive any of the four most heartbreaking crises a marriage can endure: infidelity, addiction, infertility, and loss. The stories and insights of couples who have made it through the worst will encourage you that your marriage is worth fighting for, not just because quitting is so devastating but because the rewards of sticking it out are so great.

The Parrotts explain why every marriage starts out good but inevitably bumps into bad things. Designed for use with its accompanying, individual workbooks for husbands and wives, *When Bad Things Happen to Good Marriages* could be a lifesaver for your relationship. It can make the difference between a marriage that founders on the shoals of circumstance and one that grows through hardship to release undreamed-of goodness and blessing in your lives.

Hardcover: 0-310-22459-4
Abridged Audio Pages®
   Cassette: 0-310-22977-4

Workbook for Husbands: 0-310-23902-8
Workbook for Wives: 0-310-23903-6

Pick up a copy today at your favorite bookstore!

ZONDERVAN™

GRAND RAPIDS, MICHIGAN 49530 USA

WWW.ZONDERVAN.COM

Saving Your Marriage Before It Starts

Seven Questions to Ask Before(and After) You Marry

Drs. Les & Leslie Parrott

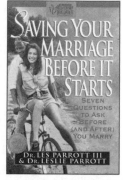

Saving Your Marriage Before It Starts is the first comprehensive marriage preparation program specifically designed for today's couples. And it's the first program for couples developed by a couple, Les and Leslie Parrott.

Having tasted firsthand the difficulties of "wedding bell blues," they show young couples the skills they need to make the transition from "single" to "married" smooth and enjoyable. Whether you're contemplating marriage, engaged, or newly married, Les and Leslie will lead you through the thorniest spot in establishing a relationship. You'll learn how to uncover and deal with problems before they emerge. You'll discover how to communicate, not just talk. And you'll learn the importance of becoming "soul mates"—a couple committed to growing together spiritually.

Hardcover: 0-310-49240-8
Leader's Guide: 0-310-20448-8
Curriculum Kit: 0-310-20451-8

Workbook for Men: 0-310-48731-5
Workbook for Women: 0-310-48741-2

Saving Your Second Marriage Before It Starts

Nine Questions to Ask Before (and After) You Remarry

Drs. Les & Leslie Parrott

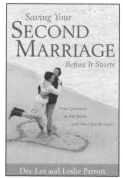

Sixty percent of second marriages fail. Yours can be among the ones that succeed. Relationship experts Les and Leslie Parrott show how you can beat the odds with flying colors and make remarriage the best thing that's ever happened to you. Do you have the skills you need? Now is the time to acquire them—and build a future together that is everything marriage can and ought to be.

Hardcover: 0-310-20748-7
Workbook for Men: 0-310-24054-9
Workbook for Women: 0-310-24055-7
Abridged Audio Pages® Cassette: 0-310-24066-2

Relationships

*An Open and Honest Guide to Making Bad
Relationships Better and Good Relationships
Great*

Drs. Les & Leslie Parrott

Les and Leslie Parrott understand firsthand our
deep need for relationships; as relationship experts,
they know what it takes to build strong, lasting
bonds. In *Relationships*, the Parrotts take us below the surface to the
depths of human interaction—to the nitty-gritty realities, the ups and
downs of building vital, satisfying connections.

Hardcover: 0-310-20755-X   Audio Pages®: 0-310-22435-7
Softcover: 0-310-24266-5

Becoming Soul Mates

Cultivating Spiritual Intimacy in the Early Years of
Marriage

Drs. Les & Leslie Parrott

Every couple has a restless aching, not just to know
God individually but to experience God together.
But how do you allow God to fill the soul of your
marriage? *Becoming Soul Mates* gives you a road
map for cultivating rich spiritual intimacy in your
relationship.

Hardcover: 0-310-20014-8   Softcover: 0-310-21926-4

Questions Couples Ask

Answers to the Top 100 Marital Questions

Drs. Les & Leslie Parrott

From communication, conflict, and careers *Questions Couples Ask* is your first resource for help
with the foremost hurdles of marriage. Drs. Les and
Leslie Parrott share cutting-edge insights on the 100
top questions married couples ask.

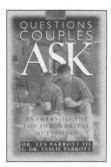

Softcover: 0-310-20754-1

Love Is. . .

Meditations for Couples on I Corinthians 13

Drs. Les & Leslie Parrott

No words, no passage, no song, no poem in all of human history has crystallized the qualities of love into simple absolutes more elegantly than 1 Corinthians 13. The Love Chapter of the Bible paints a perfect picture of love. It reveals the ideal love for which everyone yearns. But the passage is not a fantasy of what might be nice. It is a serious essay on how love can be lived, describing qualities ordinary people can cultivate to build extraordinary relationships.

Hardcover: 0-310-21666-4

Meditations on Proverbs for Couples

Drs. Les & Leslie Parrott

If yours could be the ideal marriage, what would it look like? Would it be one where hearts are open? Where faith is shared, personal growth is encouraged, dreams are nurtured, individual strengths are appreciated, romance flourishes, and even fights lead to deeper care and understanding? You can have such a marriage . . . when you build it on wisdom.

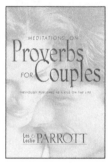

Hardcover: 0-310-23446-8

Joy Breaks for Couples

Devotions to Celebrate Marriage

Drs. Les & Leslie Parrott

Could your marriage use a joy break? Take one today! What *Joy Breaks* has done for women of faith, *Joy Breaks for Couples* does for you and your mate. These crisp devotions are brief enough to read in a few minutes, but they pack wisdom that can strengthen and energize your marriage. They'll help you see yourself, your spouse, and married life through the lens of the Bible.

Hardcover: 0-310-23122-1

Helping the Struggling Adolescent

A Guide to Thirty-Six Common Problems for Counselors, Pastors, and Youth Workers

Dr. Les Parrott

Helping the Struggling Adolescent is your first resource to turn to when a teen you know is in trouble. Whether you're a youth worker, counselor, pastor, or teacher, this fast, ready reference is a compendium of insight on teen problems from abuse to violence and everything between. Help starts here for thirty-six common, critical concerns.

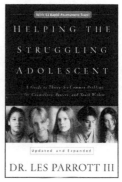

Hardcover: 0-310-23407-7

Helping Your Struggling Teenager

A Parenting Handbook on Thirty-Six Common Problems

Dr. Les Parrott

Helping Your Struggling Teenager gives you the practical information you need as a parent on thirty-six common, critical concerns your child may face. From drug and alcohol abuse to parental divorce and premarital sex, professional Christian counselor Les Parrott gives you essential insights not only on specific issues, but also on how to offer effective help as a parent.

    Helping Your Struggling Teenager organizes and condenses insights and guidance for concerned parents into one extremely useful volume. Keep it at arm's reach for the answers you need, right when you need them.

Hardcover: 0-310-23402-6

We want to hear from you. Please send your comments about this book to us in care of zreview@zondervan.com. Thank you.

ZONDERVAN™

GRAND RAPIDS, MICHIGAN 49530 USA

WWW.ZONDERVAN.COM